ECONOMIA

The Broad Field of Economics Revealed

Kapil S. Joshi

notionpress.com

INDIA • SINGAPORE • MALAYSIA

Contents

Foreword 1

Economics encompasses more than merely the analysis of wealth, markets, and commerce—it serves as a vital lens for understanding the functioning and flourishing of individuals, societies, and nations. In our globally interconnected environment, the field has broadened to tackle intricate issues like environmental sustainability, political power dynamics, human behavior, and cultural influences. ECONOMIA offers a thorough yet approachable exploration of these varied themes, presenting a comprehensive look at both foundational principles and innovative theories that are reshaping contemporary economics.

The book starts by establishing a strong groundwork through Microeconomics and Macroeconomics, the fundamental elements of the discipline. Microeconomics looks at how individuals and businesses decide on resource distribution, while macroeconomics focuses on the larger forces that impact national and global economies. Together, these concepts provide the essential knowledge needed to grasp the interaction between individual choices and collective outcomes, enabling readers to engage with more complex topics.

Moving beyond these foundational ideas, the book investigates emerging fields that mirror the changing landscape of economics. Behavioral Economics questions the traditional belief that individuals always make rational choices, illustrating how biases, emotions, and cognitive shortcuts affect decision-making. Since economic behavior can be fundamentally unpredictable, this area provides important insights into consumer behavior, market trends, and financial patterns. In parallel, Environmental Economics highlights the necessity for sustainable development, stressing the critical need to harmonize economic advancement with ecological preservation. As global issues such as climate change pose threats to long-term stability, this section underscores the importance of policies that align economic objectives with environmental considerations.

A significant asset of ECONOMIA is its focus on Political Economics, which investigates the connections between governance, power frameworks, and economic results. Policies and political choices impact various areas, from taxation and trade to income distribution and public investments. This perspective aids readers in comprehending how economics and politics converge, unveiling the reasons behind the success or failure of certain policies and how power relations shape growth and inequality.

The book also provides a historical overview of the Evolution of Economics, outlining the intellectual progression of the field through various economic schools of thought. By tracing the journey from classical to neoclassical approaches, and from Keynesian theories to modern perspectives, readers understand how economic concepts have adapted to shifting social, political, and technological landscapes. This section emphasizes economics as a fluid discipline—one that evolves over time to address societal needs.

What sets this work apart from traditional economics texts is its examination of lesser-known and unconventional theories that challenge standard viewpoints. The Kalecki Principle draws attention to how political factors impact employment and income distribution, an area often neglected in typical macroeconomic discussions. The Paradox of Thrift, which offers a counterintuitive warning that excessive saving during economic downturns can hinder recovery, teaches a vital lesson about balancing individual caution with communal prosperity.

Another fascinating aspect is the inclusion of Chaos Theory in Economics, which illustrates that economic systems can be unpredictable and nonlinear, exhibiting sensitivity to minor changes that may lead to unexpected results. This viewpoint mirrors the reality of complex markets, where small incidents can cause significant disruptions. Such perspectives are particularly relevant in a time characterized by swift technological advancements and interconnected global economies.

Additionally, the book explores Institutional Economics and Evolutionary Economics, two domains that highlight the importance of institutions and adaptation. Institutional Economics looks at how rules, norms, and governance structures influence economic behavior, offering insights into long-term development and social transformation. In contrast, Evolutionary Economics considers economies as dynamic systems that evolve through competition, innovation, and adaptation, presenting a refreshing viewpoint on how economic structures change over time.

One of the most stimulating parts of the book is its examination of Religion and Economics. Religion, typically seen as separate from conventional economics, significantly impacts societal values, ethical standards, and financial behaviors. From philanthropy to principled business practices, religion subtly yet powerfully shapes economic actions and policy choices. This analysis expands the reader's perspective on economics, illustrating how spiritual and cultural factors intertwine with material wealth.

The book offers an in-depth look at India's economy, concentrating on the hurdles and prospects encountered by one of the globe's most vibrant nations. By analyzing current strategies and future plans.

A particularly innovative element of ECONOMIA is the proposal of Wildlife-Integrated Economic Theory, reflecting a rising recognition of the connection between human economies and ecosystems.

Progress in the economy must not come at the cost of biodiversity and environmental integrity. This theory advocates for a transition towards a more comprehensive approach to development, one that incorporates wildlife preservation and ecological health into economic planning. It represents a forward-looking and creative mindset, urging readers to reconsider the dynamics between economic structures and the natural environment.

In an era where economies grow more interconnected, volatile, and environmentally challenged, this book delivers essential clarity and perspective. It motivates readers to consider unconventional models and explore a range of economic notions that capture the complexities of today's world. The blend of theory, historical context, and practical examples ensures that ECONOMIA is both enlightening and motivating, empowering readers to comprehend and influence the economic realities surrounding them.

Whether you're a student, policymaker, academic, or an interested reader, this book will provoke your thoughts and expand your outlook. It provides the means to engage thoughtfully with economic topics, fostering critical thinking and innovative solutions. The inclusion of both core ideas and unique theories guarantees that the material stays pertinent, bridging the divide between scholarly discussion and real-world application.

Anish A. Khanapurkar
Chartered Accountant

Foreword 2

The author successfully makes the 1st readers travelers through the routine branches of Economics leaving no stone unturned to touch each and every aspect of Economics.

Economia is indeed a complete guide for the beginners as well as for layman for getting a descent know of modern day Economics. Also given a insight on how India can adopt the various measures implemented by other countries in making our country more robust and strong.

The author in his first book itself has raised the expectations of the readers with such a brilliant piece of information.

Poorva Avalaskar
Assistant manager IDBI Bank Ltd

Preface

Unveiling the Essence of Economics

Economics is more than numbers, graphs, and policies—it is the study of life itself. At its core, economics explores how individuals, societies, and nations navigate the challenge of limited resources to meet unlimited wants. Its implications are vast, encompassing politics, culture, behaviour, institutions, and even the environment. In this book, *ECONOMIA*, we embark on a journey through the expansive landscape of economics, blending foundational concepts with innovative and lesser-known ideas, while applying these theories to pressing real-world issues.

This book opens with an exploration of **Microeconomics** and **Macroeconomics**, the twin pillars of economic theory. Microeconomics delves into individual and business-level decision-making, revealing how personal choices ripple out to impact markets. Macroeconomics, on the other hand, scales these concepts up, examining national and global economic systems to understand phenomena like inflation, unemployment, and international trade. Together, they provide the foundational framework for understanding both the intricate details and overarching dynamics of economic systems.

We then step into the realm of **Behavioral Economics**, where psychology meets economics. This field acknowledges that human beings are not always rational actors and explores how biases, emotions, and cognitive limitations shape economic decisions. Adjacent to this is **Environmental Economics**, a vital subject in today's world, as it seeks to reconcile economic growth with environmental sustainability. By addressing resource allocation and environmental impact, this discipline provides a roadmap for building a greener, more sustainable future.

The political dimensions of economics come alive in **Political Economics**, which reveals how power dynamics and policy decisions shape economic outcomes. From taxation and government spending to international agreements, the interplay between politics and economics is crucial for understanding the systems we live in.

Diving deeper, *ECONOMIA* ventures into unconventional and thought-provoking territories, such as the **Evolution of Economics** and **Other Economic Theories**. These sections explore how the field has grown from classical ideas to modern complexities, covering concepts like Chaos Theory, Institutional Economics, and the transformative shifts brought about by revolutions and crises. Here, readers will also encounter intriguing paradoxes, such as how individual savings behavior can collectively destabilize an economy.

In a unique addition, the book examines **Religion and Economics**, shedding light on how religious values and practices influence economic systems and decision-making. This chapter bridges the gap between two seemingly distinct realms, offering fresh perspectives on economic behavior.

One of the most exciting aspects of *ECONOMIA* is its focus on India, a nation at the forefront of economic transformation. The chapter on **Developing and Growing India's Economy** presents an in-depth analysis of current strategies and future opportunities. It highlights India's journey toward sustainable growth, technological innovation, and global competitiveness, offering valuable insights for policymakers, entrepreneurs, and citizens alike.

Finally, the book concludes with **Wildlife-Integrated Economic Theory (WET)**, a novel perspective that integrates ecological conservation with economic development, showcasing a harmonious approach to growth and biodiversity.

Whether you are a student, professional, or simply curious about the forces shaping our world, *ECONOMIA* equips you with the knowledge to navigate the intricate and dynamic field of economics. This well written book by Kapil S. Joshi is not just an academic endeavour—it is an invitation to think critically about the choices we make and their impact on our shared future.

With best wishes:
Dr. Swami Shailendra Saraswati
Shree Rajneesh Dhyan Mandir
Deepalpur, Distt: Sonipat (HR)

Acknowledgement

I am deeply grateful to the numerous individuals who have supported me throughout this journey, without whom this book would not have been possible.

First and foremost, I would like to express my heartfelt appreciation to my family (Especially my mother Mrs. Revati S. Joshi), whose unwavering encouragement and patience have been my driving force.

For the Preface

1. Dr. Swami Shailendra Saraswati younger brother of Acharya Rajneesh Osho and founder of Osho fragrance: Your deep understanding and knowledge, based on the teachings, have significantly enhanced this book. I am greatful for your involvement.

For the Foreword

1. Mr. Anish A. Khanapurkar (CA): Your expertise and thoughtful reflections have added significant depth to this book. Thank you for sharing your valuable perspectives

2. Mrs. Poorva Avalaskar (Assistant Manager, IDBI Bank Ltd): Your thoughtful words have enriched this book. I appreciate your time and consideration.

To my esteemed colleagues, Mr. Mandar Pingale and Ms. Hrujuta Widhvans, and mentors, thank you for your invaluable guidance, expertise, and inspiration.

To my community and Mr. Madhav Dakave for digital photograph.

My profound appreciation also goes out to five wonderful people who were once my pupils and whose commitment, curiosity, and excitement have always served as a source of inspiration: Mr. Sujal S. Gangan, Ms. Arfiya A. Kondivkar, Ms. Huda Shiekhnag, Ms. Shruti G. Purohit and Ms. Nida I. Khedekar.

I am grateful to have been a part of your academic career and have been deeply impacted by your scholarly curiosity and rigor.

To the entire Notion Press team, thank you for your professionalism, support, and commitment to bringing this project to fruition.

Lastly, I would like to acknowledge the countless researchers, scholars, and thinkers whose work has informed and shaped my ideas. Your contributions have enriched my understanding and inspired me to contribute to the ongoing conversation.

Thank you all for your contributions, guidance, and encouragement.

Sincerely,

Kapil S. Joshi

Introduction

At its essence, Economics examines the choices made by individuals, societies, and nations when faced with limited resources. Its influence extends beyond mere financial transactions and statistics, shaping politics, behaviour, institutions, and even the environment. ECONOMIA guides its readers through the expansive realm of economics, blending foundational theories with uncommon, thought-provoking ideas and applying them to real-world issues, including the economic development of India.

The journey commences with the fundamental principles of Microeconomics and Macroeconomics, the building blocks of economic theory. Microeconomics investigates the decision-making processes of individuals and businesses, while Macroeconomics extends this analysis to encompass national and global economic phenomena. Together, these frameworks form the basis for comprehending everything from household finances to international trade and government policies.

Subsequently, the book explores Behavioural Economics, an area that challenges traditional economic models by integrating human psychology into economic analysis. Recognising that people are not always rational decision-makers, this field examines how biases and emotions influence economic choices. Complementing this is Environmental Economics, which tackles the urgent question of how economies can develop sustainably while balancing growth with the responsible use of the Earth's resources.

Political Economics introduces a crucial dimension by revealing the interconnectedness of power, policy, and economics. Governments play a pivotal role in shaping economic outcomes, and this field investigates the interplay between political forces and economic performance.

Going beyond conventional theories, ECONOMIA introduces readers to rare and intriguing concepts. Chaos Theory explores the unpredictable nature of economies, where small changes can lead to significant disruptions. Institutional Economics emphasises the significance of social and legal institutions in shaping economic outcomes, while Revolutionary Economics explores how economies undergo transformative shifts during periods of upheaval. The Paradox of Thrift presents a counterintuitive lesson on how personal saving habits can sometimes harm, rather than help, an economy.

Religion also influences economic behaviour. In a dedicated chapter on Religion & Economics, the book examines how religious beliefs, values, and structures impact economic systems and decisions.

Finally, ECONOMIA focuses on Developing and Growing India's Economy: Present Strategies and Upcoming Courses. As one of the world's largest and most dynamic economies, India is charting a course towards sustainable growth, technological innovation, and global competitiveness. This section highlights key policies, strategies, and future challenges as India strives to realise its economic potential.

ECONOMIA provides readers with a comprehensive perspective on economics, blending traditional and modern theories with unique insights into India's future. Whether you are a student, professional, or simply curious about how the world works, this book equips you with the tools to comprehend the intricate and ever-evolving field of economics.

What's Economics?

The production, distribution, and consumption of products and services are the primary subjects of examination inside the social science of economics. The principal focus of the study of economics is on the decisions that human beings, companies, governments, and international locations make about how to divide up scarce resources.

Comprehending Economics

Under the assumption that human goals are boundless in a world of finite resources, economists study the distribution of resources through production, consumption, and distribution.

Economic Indicators: What Are They?

Economic indicators provide specifics on the state of an economic system. Economic indicators are often released on a regular basis by public or private entities, and they frequently have a significant impact on international markets, employment, and equities. They can foresee future economic trends that will impact markets and direct investment decisions.

What Role Does an Economist Serve?

Economic regulations pertaining to interest rates, tax policies, employment programmes, global trade agreements, and company strategy are formed by economists, who study the relationship between a society's resources and production or output. To identify potential trends or create economic projections, economists study economic data like the consumer price index and the gross domestic product.

Three-quarters of all American economists, according to the Bureau of Labor Statistics (BLS), are employed by federal or state governments. In addition, economists work for companies as lecturers, consultants, or as members of think tanks focused on economic issues.

Fundamental Ideas in Economics

The examine of economics examines how humans, agencies, governments, and groups distribute finite assets to fulfill limitless needs and wants. Microeconomics and macroeconomics make up its two primary branches. Macroeconomics studies the economy as a whole, searching at huge-scale monetary factors like inflation, unemployment, and country-wide output, even as microeconomics concentrates on individual decision-making units like houses and businesses.

Scarcity and choice: The theory of scarcity, which holds that human dreams are limitless however assets (such as time, money, hard work, and herbal sources) are finite, is essential to economics. humans and societies are compelled by using shortage to make choices at the best use in their sources. opportunity value, or the well worth of the next first-rate option given up whilst making a decision, is a component of every selection. for example, the government can also lose out on funding for infrastructure or schooling if it spends money on healthcare.

Supply and Demand: In a market financial system, the connection between delivery and demand is important in setting prices. The quantity of an item or carrier that clients are willing and able to buy at distinct pricing is referred to as demand. The amount that manufacturers are inclined and able to promote at numerous costs is referred to as the supply. In step with the rule of demand, the amount preferred for an object rises when its fee lowers and vice versa, all different things being the same. In a similar vein, the regulation of delivery states that a growth in rate corresponds to a growth in the quantity introduced. While the amount supplied and demanded are the same, the marketplace rate and amount exchanged are at equilibrium.

Opportunity Cost: Possibility value is the next high-quality option given up while selecting a choice, as changed into previously mentioned. Know-how exchange-offs require an understanding of this idea. For instance, the opportunity fee of a business generating motors as opposed to vans is the vehicles that would have been produced. The misplaced enjoyment time is the opportunity value of private decisions like determining to work in place of unwind.

Marginal Analysis: Marginal analysis is a tool used by economists to examine choice-making on the margins. This involves assessing the greater or incremental charges and blessings of a route of movement. A company can inquire, "what is the extra gain of manufacturing one more unit of a product in comparison to the extra value?" as an instance. The ideal level of output or intake, where marginal profits equal marginal prices, is ascertained with the use of this study.

Efficiency and Equity: In economics, efficiency is the high-quality use of assets to maximize welfare and productivity. Allocative efficiency, wherein sources are allocated in accordance with client alternatives, and effective performance, wherein goods and services are produced at the lowest possible price, are the two principal classes of performance. But, an affordable and equitable distribution of resources is not continually the end result of monetary performance. The equity of monetary effects is a problem with fairness. Performance and fairness are regularly trade-offs for policymakers, as increasing economic equity (for example, through redistributive measures) can sometimes lower efficiency by warping incentives.

Markets and Government: The main tool used to coordinate economic activities is the marketplace. Prices function as alerts in a loose marketplace to facilitate the effective allocation of assets, but there are some reasons why markets can fail, including monopolies (when one organization controls a marketplace), public goods (which are non-excludable and non-rivalrous), and externalities (where costs or advantages flow to third parties). To address market imperfections and boost welfare in these situations, authorities' action might be required.

Gross Domestic Product (GDP): Gross domestic Product (GDP) is the main indicator of a country's monetary output at the macroeconomic level. The entire marketplace value of all completed products and services produced in a state over a particular time period is represented through the GDP. It serves as a gauge for the growth and well-being of a country's financial system. A better understanding of output fluctuations over the years is offered through real GDP, which accounts for inflation.

Inflation and Unemployment: The charge at which prices for goods and services are commonly growing and reducing buying power is called inflation. Economic policy is utilized by central banks, along with the Federal Reserve within the USA and the Reserve bank of India, to manipulate inflation. The fraction of the workforce that is unemployed but actively searching for work is called the unemployment rate. Low unemployment usually denotes a strong economy, but high unemployment can result in societal problems and the underuse of resources.

Microeconomics

In relation to behaviour and decisions, Macroeconomics research the financial system as an entire, while Microeconomics concentrates on the actions and choices of individual units, which include homes, agencies, and industries. So, one can allocate sources inside a market and react to changes in pricing, delivery, and demand. Microeconomics research how these entities interact. Due to its ability to make clear the fundamental ideas underlying extra preferred financial actions, this location of economics is taken into consideration as foundational.

They look at monetary hobbies in the person or micro stage, which is called microeconomics. It appears on the picks that groups, industries, and character customers make approximately how nice to distribute items and offerings and allocate resources, which will shape marketplace outcomes. Microeconomics also examines how these human beings and organizations react to incentives, the results of policies, and marketplace imperfections.

Scope:

Demand and Supply Analysis: Understanding how the quantity and fee of objects are decided with the aid of marketplace call for and supply.

Consumer Behavior: Examining how people pick what to devour in reaction to incentives, barriers, and possibilities.

Production and Costs: Gaining knowledge of the way businesses choose their output extent, production methods, and input mixtures if you want to cut costs and boom earnings.

Market Structures: Analyzing the diverse market paperwork ideal, Monopolistic, Oligopolistic, and Monopoly and the way they affect aid allocation and price.

Factor Markets: Examining the markets for capital, exertions, and different requirements for manufacturing.

Welfare Economics: Assessing the effectiveness and fairness of diverse marketplace results as well as the effects of governmental moves.

The 10 Principles of Microeconomics

The fundamental ideas behind understanding how economies operate at the micro level are found in the principles of microeconomics, which were developed by economist N. Gregory Mankiw.

How People Make Decisions

People Face Trade-offs: Economics is the examine of scarce assets and decision-making with the aid of people. There are always trade-offs whilst allocating assets in one region, for example, procuring a ride could cut into the amount of money left over for future purchases.

The Cost of Something is What You Give Up to Get It: The opportunity fee precept states that the authentic cost of something includes the sacrifices required to comply with a selected route of action. For instance, the value of attending college consists of both the tuition and the wages lost from not working.

Rational People Think at the Margin: Marginal evaluation is the manner through which rational human beings weigh the multiplied gain of a preference in opposition to its greater rate. For example, in the event that the marginal gain outweighs the marginal fee, a business enterprise will produce one extra unit of the good.

People Respond to Incentives: Rewards are critical in influencing conduct. Fees affect purchasers; however, corporations react to possibilities for earnings. Taxes and subsidies are equipment used by policymakers to shape market behavior.

How People Interact With Each Other

Trade Can Make Everyone Better Off: Trade raises living standards by allowing humans and groups to focus on their areas of knowledge and exchange goods and services with others.

Markets Are Usually a Good Way to Organize Economic Activity: In marketplace economies, the distribution of resources is decided by way of the interplay among consumers and dealers. Markets that are running successfully usually distribute resources in a manner that maximises wealth.

Governments Can Sometimes Improve Market Outcomes: Externalities (consisting of pollutants) or the life of public items (which include countrywide safety) would possibly cause markets to fail. In a few conditions, government motion through law or the provision of precise merchandise may additionally enhance wellness generally.

The Forces and Trends That Affect How the Economy as a Whole Works

A Country's Standard of Living Depends on Its Ability to Produce Goods and Services: Increasing living standards are an end result of increasing productivity. Greater productive international locations can afford greater levels of services and spending.

Prices Rise When the Government Prints Too Much Money: the money supply expands greater fast than the provision of products and offerings, inflation results. This concept links financial policy and macroeconomic balance.

Society Faces a Short-Run Trade-off Between Inflation and Unemployment: Inflation and unemployment regularly alternate inside the brief term, particularly at some point of times of economic growth or contraction. In step with this concept, controlling inflation may additionally sometimes result in higher unemployment and vice versa.

Essential Ideas in Microeconomics

Demand and Supply: The connection among demand and supply, which establishes the marketplace charge and quantity of products, is the primary guiding principle of microeconomics. In keeping with the law of demand, amount preferred for an item decreases as its fee increases, all other things being identical. Alternatively, according to the rule of thumb of supply, the amount supplied of an item rises as its price does.

Elasticity: The degree to which the amount provided or required of an object responds to fee fluctuations is called its elasticity. A small change in price will result in a great alteration in the quantity supplied or required if the good is price elastic. Groups can better understand pricing tactics and client sensitivity to price fluctuations with the aid of utilizing elasticity.

Consumer Surplus and Producer Surplus: The gap between what clients are prepared to pay and what they actually pay for a commodity is referred to as the consumer surplus. The difference between what producers are inclined to sell a good for and the fee they receive is referred to as the manufacturer surplus. When combined, they calculate the welfare advantages of market exchanges.

Production and Costs: A corporation's purpose is to maximize profits while minimizing prices. The price systems constant, variable, and total prices have an effect on how much a corporation will generate. Whilst making manufacturing selections, agencies weigh the extra expense of creating a single unit in opposition to the marginal sales. This is called the marginal cost.

Perfect Competition vs. Monopoly: Every seller and each buyer have identical market strength in a very competitive market in which all commodities are the same. A monopoly, alternatively, results from one corporation controlling the market; this typically drives up prices and reduces output. The examination of microeconomics examines the benefits of aggressive marketplaces in addition to the inefficiencies in monopolistic ones.

Game Theory: A subfield of economics referred to as "game theory" examines strategic interactions in which every player's final result is dependent on the actions of others. When examining oligopolistic markets—markets wherein a small number of dominant businesses exert interdependent impact over each other—it is especially pertinent.

Market Failures: The inefficiency of markets in allocating assets can be attributed to public goods, externalities, and facts asymmetry. Microeconomics investigates those shortcomings and how the government might be capable of dealing with them. One poor externality that leads to an excess of harmful products produced is pollution.

Welfare Economics: The situation of welfare economics seems at how resource distribution affects humans' economic protection. It evaluates numerous marketplace effects using ideas like Pareto efficiency, which holds that no one can get better off without making someone else worse off.

Labour and Capital Markets: In order to better apprehend how wages, employment, and returns on capital are hooked up in these respective markets, microeconomics also examines the supply and demand of labour and capital.

Public Goods and Common Resources: Common resources (rivalrous however non-excludable, like fisheries) and public items (non-excludable and non-rivalrous, like national security) provide unique challenges given that markets have a tendency to overuse commonplace resources and underproduce public goods in the absence of government movement.

Market Structure in Microeconomics

A key concept in microeconomics, marketplace structure explains the composition and trends of numerous marketplaces in an economy. It addresses how businesses characteristic in admire to choices regarding pricing, manufacturing, and competition. As it allows economists and policymakers to forecast organization conduct, market performance, customer welfare, and general economic outcomes, information on a market's structure is critical. Market systems can be categorized into four predominant classes: oligopoly, monopoly, ideal opposition, and monopolistic opposition. The number of corporations within the marketplace, the styles of merchandise offered, the diploma of competition, and the benefit of getting into and leaving the marketplace decide how each structure is one of a kind.

Perfect Competition

An idealized marketplace gadget with many tiny agencies competing against each other is referred to as perfect competition. In this case, each employer sells the same (homogeneous) merchandise, and no single firm has the power to affect a product's price.

Characteristics:

Massive range of consumers and sellers: each firm in the market contributes only a small portion of the full supply. As price takers, buyers and dealers accept the going rate inside the market without trying to force it higher or lower.

Homogeneous merchandise: All companies offer almost the same or similar items. Customers do not express a preference for one firm over another as a result.

Ideal facts: All producers and consumers are fully aware of the terms of the market, including product availability, quality, and prices.

Unrestricted access and exit: There are no significant barriers to entry or exiting the market, including expensive startup costs or complex regulations.

Price-taking behaviour: The dynamics of supply and demand determine the marketplace price because no company has enough marketplace power to influence it.

Because firms produce at the point where marginal cost (MC) equals marginal revenue (MR), which is also equal to the marketplace fee, they can operate at ideal performance in a totally aggressive marketplace. In the long run, agencies make typical income because abnormal gains could attract new competition and lower fees. For example, one of the most common examples of close to-perfect opposition within the real world is agriculture. Comparable crops are produced by many farmers, and no farmer has the power to affect the price of wheat or maize available on the market.

Monopoly

A monopoly is a type of market structure in which single firm controls the whole market and is the only one offering goods or services. The monopolist in this case has substantial control over the product's price.

Characteristics:

Single seller: A single firm has complete control over all of a product's supply on the market.

Unique product: The monopolist's product has no close substitutes, which allows the company to have significant pricing control.

Barriers to entry: High entry barriers – which might be brought about by economies of scale, control over vital resources, legal constraints (such as patents), or governmental regulations – are the reason monopolies arise.

Price maker: In contrast to businesses operating in complete competition, monopolists set prices. Due to the lack of direct competition, it can set prices higher than the marginal cost.

A common criticism of monopolies is their inefficiency. Producing at a level where marginal revenue equals marginal cost – a level below what would be generated in a competitive market—allows a monopolist to maximise profit. Monopolies may therefore result in less consumer surplus and higher pricing. Furthermore, since monopolies are not subject to competition pressure, they can be less motivated to develop or enhance their products. For instance, A local utility firm that supplies water or power to a particular area is a prime example of a monopoly. A single company controls the majority of the market since it is frequently impractical for several businesses to compete due to the high cost of infrastructure.

Monopolistic Competition

In a marketplace structure called monopolistic competition, several corporations compete with each other while presenting fairly one-of-a-kind products. This arrangement blends elements of monopoly and perfect competition.

Characteristics:

Large number of firms: Notwithstanding the reality that there are numerous businesses in the market, each agency has some diploma of marketplace strength due to product differentiation.

Product differentiation: Groups sell similar yet distinct products. A few examples of differentiators are quality, branding, and customer service.

Free access and exit: Agencies can enter or exit the marketplace as an alternative simply, just like in an excellent competition.

Fee-setting ability: Due to the fact all agency›s services are unique, it has some control over the pricing of its product. The degree of control is still constrained by the availability of alternatives.

When there is monopolistic competition, groups make ordinary earnings over the long time for the reason that newly joining the marketplace reduces any anomalous brief-term income. Businesses compete on the premise of non-rate elements such client loyalty, product characteristics, and advertising as well as price. Monopolistic opposition has a tendency to be less efficient than best opposition because of the differentiated nature of the gadgets, but it offers clients more choice. For instance, one marketplace in which monopolistic opposition is evident is the eating place industry. At the same time as many eating places have identical menus and meal services, what sets them aside from rivals is their ingesting revel in, menu, or area.

Oligopoly

A market shape known as an oligopoly is defined with the aid of some dominant most important firms in the marketplace. These corporations may additionally act strategically to have an effect on marketplace outcomes considering they have got a variety of marketplace strength.

Characteristics:

Few corporations: Maximum market percentage is managed with the aid of a restricted quantity of agencies.

Interdependence: In an oligopoly, businesses rely heavily on each other. The decisions made via rival corporations may be greatly impacted by the sports of one employer (e.g., pricing modifications, new product introductions).

Boundaries to entry: High access boundaries prevent new organizations from joining the marketplace easily. Examples of those hurdles include economies of scale, massive capital requirements, or get entry to generation.

Non-fee competition: This will save you price wars. Agencies running in oligopolies often compete via non-charge means like branding, marketing, and product differentiation.

Collusion and cooperation: Groups running in an oligopoly can also sometimes have interaction in overt or covert collusion to decide charges and increase usual profits. Such behaviour can result in systems similar to cartels.

Patron charges will increase, and market inefficiencies can result from oligopolies, particularly if agencies band collectively to stifle competition.

To achieve an edge over competitors, oligopolies may also, despite the fact that, from time to time, compete on fees or make sizable investments in new products and innovation development. For instance, an oligopoly is satisfactory, as shown by the car area. The global marketplace is ruled by the aid of a few huge manufacturers, including Ford, Widespread Motors, and Toyota. Those groups compete fiercely, but they also have an impact on one another.

In the end, A foundation for comprehending how corporations and markets paint is furnished by market structures in microeconomics. Each shape—oligopoly, monopoly, monopolistic opposition, and ideal competition—has particular developments that have an effect on pricing policies, corporate behaviour, and the general effectiveness of the market. While oligopolies and monopolies can result in inefficiencies and lower patron welfare, perfect competition produces the maximum efficient marketplace effects. Even though it offers stability by bearing in mind a range of products, monopolistic opposition is typically less effective than ideal opposition. Economists, choice-makers, and corporations ought to recognize those marketplace structures so they can make properly knowledgeable choices that affect the welfare of the economy.

Game Theory in Microeconomics

A framework known as "game theory" is used to analyze and simulate strategic interactions among human beings or businesses wherein every player's result relies on their own and different people's choices. The game idea is useful in microeconomics to understand quite a number of market phenomena, along with cooperation and competition as well as oligopolistic behavior and bargaining.

Basics of Game Theory

The study of strategic interactions, in which dealers or organizations make selections based on how exceptional to maximize their payoffs, is referred to as recreation idea. In sport concept, the critical components of any recreation are:

Players: The folks who make the decisions, who can be agencies, people, or different monetary agents.

Techniques: The range of alternatives to be had to every participant.

Payoffs: The effects or incentives that gamers gain by combining their selected strategies. statistics: whether or not gamers realize the strategies and payoffs of different players flawlessly (absolutely) or imperfectly (incompletely).

Equilibrium: The final results of the sport in which no participant has any motivation to regulate their approach on their own.

Types of Games

Game theory deals with numerous game genres, each having precise properties:

Simultaneous vs. Sequential video games: In sequential video games, gamers take turns and few understand the earlier movements of others, but in simultaneous video games, gamers make choices concurrently without understanding what the other players have executed.

Zero-Sum vs. Non-Zero-Sum Games: In non-zero-sum games, both participants may win or lose, however in zero-sum games, one player's gain is another player's loss.

Cooperative vs. Non-Cooperative Games: Cooperative games allow participants to join coalitions and negotiate enforceable agreements, whereas non-cooperative games do not.

Nash Equilibrium

John Nash established one of the most important notions in game theory, the Nash equilibrium. A Nash equilibrium is a condition in which each player chooses their optimal strategy based on the tactics of the others, and no player benefits by altering their plan unilaterally.

For instance, in the well-known Prisoner's Dilemma, two inmates are apprehended for a crime and are faced with the choice of confessing or staying silent. They both get short sentences if they don't say anything. One is set free if they confess while the other remains mute; the silent person receives a severe punishment. Both receive moderate punishments if they both confess. Although both convicts confess, the Nash equilibrium is reached since neither party benefits from making a unilateral change in course, even although keeping quiet would have produced a better result for the group as a whole.

Dominant Strategies

Any strategy that gives a player a larger payout irrespective of what the other players do is considered dominant. The sport is said to have a dominant method equilibrium if every participant has a dominant method.

As an example, within the Prisoner's dilemma, both prisoners want to confess since, in all instances, doing so results in a better or equal outcome than remaining silent, regardless of the other prisoner's preference.

Applications of Game Theory

Oligopoly

In microeconomics, analysing oligopolistic markets—in which a small range of rather interdependent businesses dominate the marketplace—is one of the most significant applications of game theory. Oligopolistic companies often need to make strategic decisions about product differentiation, output levels, and prices.

The Cournot model is a well-known oligopoly theory model in which firms concurrently decide how much output to generate while taking their competitors' output decisions into consideration. When no firm is able to improve its profit by unilaterally adjusting its output level, the firms attain a Nash equilibrium.

The Bertrand version, wherein businesses compete on pricing in place of amount, is another pertinent model. In this example, organizations frequently reduce costs until they reach the marginal value pricing Nash equilibrium, at which neither commercial enterprise can cut expenses any further without incurring losses.

Price Wars and Collusion

Businesses in oligopolies may additionally wage charge wars which will gain marketplace proportion. Game concept affords an explanation for why fee wars can manifest and how they can have bad results on all events concerned. A company may additionally reduce its rate in a sequential game of charge competition in the hopes that its competitor would follow in shape. This "tit-for-tat" method can also cause the profitability of each business to decline.

Auctions

The analysis of numerous public sale codecs, wherein members bid on services or products, is a commonplace software of recreation idea. In those strategic video games of chance, the item of every provide is to outbid the opposing bidder without going over finances.

Two common types of auctions are:

First-price sealed-bid auctions: The highest bidder wins but must pay the quantity they bid after individuals put up sealed bids. Whilst taking competing bids into consideration, the best course of action is often to bid much less than the maximum amount that the player is prepared to spend.

Second-price sealed-bid auctions (Vickrey auctions): The prevailing bidder can pay the second-maximum quantity, however additionally they win. Since the winner can pay less than or identical to their appraisal, bidding one's proper value is the prevailing technique in this instance.

Public Goods and Free-Rider Problem

Game theory examines the loose-rider hassle within the setting of non-excludable and non-rivalrous public goods. People are inspired to take advantage of the public trust without assisting to fund it, which leads to underinvestment in the good. In a collective action recreation, strategic interactions can bring about the supply of public goods that is not most useful, and the improvement of incentives for voluntary contributions or authorities' intervention are frequently used as remedies.

Repeated Games and the Folk Theorem

Players can establish reputations and penalize or reward others depending on their previous behavior by interacting with each other several times in repeated games. Cooperation can occur in these kinds of games even when there isn't a Nash equilibrium after one play. In a recurrent prisoner's dilemma, for instance, participants might initially collaborate, but if one cheats, the other might revenge in subsequent rounds.

According to the Folk Theorem, an expansion of outcomes, including cooperative ones, may be sustained as equilibria in infinitely repeated games, contingent on the strategies hired with the aid of the gamers and their discounting of destiny payoffs. This is especially important in sectors where organizations have interaction with one another on a everyday basis, enabling processes like rate matching or implicit collusion.

Limitations

Information asymmetry: Predictions are made more difficult in real-global eventualities while there may be regularly insufficient or inaccurate records.

Multiple equilibria: It may be challenging to decide which of numerous Nash equilibria in a sport will finally emerge.

Behavioral assumptions: Despite the fact that game theory presupposes rational behaviour, human beings and companies can also behave irrationally or in step with restricted rationality in real life.

To sum up, In microeconomics, game theory is an important device for comprehending strategic interactions in marketplaces characterized via interdependence, cooperation, and competition. It offers perceptions into public goods, auctions, oligopolies, and routine interactions, assisting economists and policymakers in forecasting results and growing more effective structures to guarantee effective market behavior. Nonetheless, game theory is only one component of the jigsaw with regards to comprehending real-world economics because of the assumptions of rationality and best knowledge.

Macroeconomics

Macroeconomics is a subfield of economics that specializes in a mixture of variables and huge-scale monetary troubles to look at a financial system's overall performance and functioning. Macroeconomics research the elements that have an effect on the whole economy, together with countrywide profits, overall intake, funding, inflation, unemployment, and governmental rules, whereas microeconomics makes a speciality of man or woman sellers, markets, and selections. Its objective is to realize the larger photo and offer devices for controlling the economy via financial, financial, and other rules.

Because it permits economists and choice-makers to recognize patterns and problems that have an effect on the economy as an entire, macroeconomics is crucial. This enables governments to keep economic stability, sell increases, and accomplish goals like full employment and coffee inflation by making nicely informed choices on issues like taxation, expenditure, and monetary coverage.

Scope:

National Income Accounting: Accounting for national income measures the economic activities of a nation. This entails figuring out the GDP, or gross domestic product, which is the entire worth of products and services generated inside a nation's boundaries over a given period of time. The Gross National Product (GNP), Net National Product (NNP), and Net Domestic Product (NDP) are other significant indicators. Economists and policymakers can assess the general state of the economy and its potential for expansion with the use of these indicators.

Inflation and Price Levels: In macroeconomics, inflation an increase within the average degree of costs for goods and services – is a key subject matter of study. Immoderate inflation can cause economic instability, reduce shopping power, and affect investments and savings. Deflation, alternatively, might result in reduced customer spending and investment, which is also a reason for concern. Macroeconomists study demand-pull (excessive demand) and price-push (increasing production charges) elements that contribute to inflation and provide price stability control strategies.

Unemployment: The study of macroeconomics looks into the many forms of structural, cyclical, and frictional unemployment rates. Excessive unemployment charges impede monetary growth by reflecting underuse of resources. Macroeconomists look into the origins and consequences of unemployment and create regulations intended to lower it. Economic and social effects of unemployment may include decreased consumer spending, lack of profits and opportunities, and higher government welfare prices.

Economic Growth and Development: Economic growth is the sluggish growth in a country's production of goods and offerings as indicated by shifts in real GDP. Alternatively, financial development encompasses more and consists of elevating dwelling standards, reducing poverty, and facilitating access to healthcare and education. Macroeconomists study the factors that cause sustained growth, together with capital accumulation, human capital enhancements, and technology breakthroughs. They also look at growth-restraining factors and the ways in which public policy can promote development.

Business Cycles: Business cycles, which are described as durations of expansion (increase) and contraction (recession), are the versions in monetary pastime that an economic system is going through throughout time. The purpose of macroeconomics is to recognize the factors that cause these cycles and find out strategies for lessening the damaging consequences of recessions. Manufacturing declines and unemployment rates rise during recessions, while levels of employment, income, and production all rise during expansions.

Monetary Policy and Central Banking: Managing the cash delivery and interest costs is called monetary policy, and it is accomplished by way of significant banks including the Reserve Bank with the intention to preserve currency balance, prevent inflation, and stall monetary expansion. Macroeconomists study the effects of interest price changes on inflation, consumption, and investment. To affect liquidity and monetary interest, primary banks rent instruments along with reserve requirements, the discount rate, and open market operations.

Fiscal Policy: The usage of taxation and expenditure through the authorities to have an effect on the economic system is called financial policy. Macroeconomists look at the capability effects on employment, mixture demand, and economic growth of adjustments in authorities borrowing, spending, and taxation. Whilst contractionary fiscal rules goal is to lower inflation and cool down hot economies, expansionary financial rules, such as increased government spending or tax cuts, are employed to boost the economy.

International Trade and Finance: International trade and finance also are covered by using macroeconomics, which makes a specialty of alternate prices, balances of bills, change deficits, and surpluses. It appears at how a state's trade connections with other international locations both impact and are encouraged via its financial regulations and performance. Macroeconomists look at the effects of alternate regulations, price lists, and currency values on a financial system, particularly in a world developing more closely interconnected by the day.

Macroeconomic Models: Simplified depictions of economies' workings, called macroeconomic models, enable economists to check various theories and forecast results. The Classical model, Keynesian model, and Monetarist version are some popular models that each offer a completely unique view of how economies function and react to policies. Economists can foresee future economic conditions and advocate strategies that may stabilise economies using these models.

Applications of Macroeconomics

Policy Formulation: Developing government policy is one of the most critical uses of macroeconomics. Macroeconomic principles are used within the advent of each monetary and fiscal regulation. For instance, governments may additionally use expansionary financial measures, such as extra public spending and tax breaks, to boost demand for the duration of a recession. In a comparable vein, hobby price discounts by primary banks might also promote borrowing and funding. The basis for those guidelines is provided by using macroeconomic analysis, which forecasts how exclusive variables will interact and affect the economic system as an entire.

Economic Stabilization: Macroeconomics offers instruments for overseeing monetary stability. Macroeconomists offer hints on techniques to stabilize the financial system with the aid of analysing the factors that contribute to inflation, unemployment, and monetary boom. For example, primary banks might also boom interest quotes to lower expenditure and obstruct price increases throughout times of excessive inflation. However, governments can also implement job advent tasks to boost employment ranges for the duration of times of high unemployment. Macroeconomic theories and models function as the foundation for these stabilizing strategies.

Forecasting Economic Trends: Future economic patterns can be expected with the resource of macroeconomics, that is vital for corporations and policymakers alike. Macroeconomists are able to forecast destiny monetary conditions with a high degree of accuracy by means of reading historic records on variables like GDP increase, inflation costs, and unemployment. These projections resource inside the anticipation of economic booms and downturns and are critical for corporate plans, government making plans, and investment decisions.

Global Economic Interactions: Understanding macroeconomics is vital to comprehending the worldwide interactions among economies. Macroeconomic selections made in a single country can have a huge impact on economies in different international locations while trade and finance are the primary means of financial interconnection in the international. For example, a state's trade balance and competitiveness in global markets are impacted through its exchange rate rules. A good way to preserve honest and balanced worldwide trade flows, governments and global corporations use macroeconomic analysis to govern those interactions.

Business Decision-Making: Macroeconomic analysis is a tool utilised by groups to make alternatives for lengthy periods. For instance, while thinking about expansions or investments, businesses do not forget modifications in inflation, hobby rates, and usual financial increases. Comprehending the wider economic panorama helps organisations mitigate dangers and optimise opportunities. For instance, an enterprise may additionally determine to put off fees in surroundings with high hobby charges because borrowing will become extra luxurious, or it can determine to develop for the duration of instances of economic growth while demand from clients is increasing.

Crisis Management: Macroeconomic models and techniques are even greater crucial for the duration of economic downturns, as the COVID-19 pandemic and the 2008 worldwide monetary disaster. To reduce the terrible consequences of crises, governments and principal banks enforce macroeconomic regulations like stimulus applications and quantitative easing. Macroeconomics affords measures to stabilize the financial system, increase self-belief, and forestall lengthy-term damage, supporting policymakers throughout these tumultuous times.

Essential Ideas in Macroeconomics

1. **Gross Domestic Product (GDP):** GDP is the sum of all the commodities and services produced inside a nation's boundaries over a given time period. It serves as the main metric for assessing how well a nation's economy is doing.

There are three methods to calculate GDP:

1. Expenditure Approach.
2. Income Approach.
3. Production (Value Added) Approach

However, the Expenditure Approach is the most common, and its formula is: GDP = C + I + G + (X – M)

Where:

- C = Consumption (spending by households)
- I = Investment (spending by businesses)
- G = Government expenditure
- X = Exports
- M = Imports (so X – M is net exports)

Real Vs. Nominal GDP: Nominal GDP is calculated using current prices, without taking inflation into account. With constant prices applied, real GDP accounts for inflation.

Nominal GDP to Real GDP conversion formula:

Real GDP = Nominal GDP ÷ GDP Deflator

GDP Deflator: The price level of all newly generated final products and services in an economy is measured by the GDP deflator.

Formula:

GDP Deflator = Nominal GDP ÷ Real GDP × 100.

Unemployment Rate: The unemployment rate measures the proportion of the labor force that is unemployed and actively seeking employment.

Formula:

Unemployment Rate = Number of Unemployed people ÷ Labour Force × 100

Where: Labour Force includes people who are employed and those who are actively seeking work (i.e., unemployed).

Inflation: Inflation is the rate at which the general level of prices for goods and services is rising, eroding purchasing power.

The popular method to measure inflation is the Consumer Price Index (CPI).

Formula:

CPI = Cost of Market Basket in Current Year ÷ Cost of Market Basket in Base Year × 100

To calculate the inflation rate from the CPI:

Inflation Rate: CPI Current Index – CPI Previous Year ÷ CPI Previous Year × 100

Money Supply and Velocity of Money: The velocity of money refers to how quickly money circulates in the economy, or the rate at which money changes hands. The quantity theory of money relates the money supply to the price level and economic output.

The quantity theory of money can be expressed as:

$MV = PQ$

Where:

M = Money Supply

V = Velocity of Money

P = Price Level

Q = Real Output (Real GDP)

This equation shows that the total amount of money used in purchases (MV) is equal to the nominal GDP (PQ).

Aggregate Demand (AD) and Aggregate Supply (AS): The total demand for goods and services in an economy at a specific price level is known as aggregate demand, whereas aggregate supply refers to the total output of goods and services that firms are willing to produce at a particular price level.

The formula for Aggregate Demand (AD) is:

$$AD = C + I + G + (X - M).$$

The components in the GDP formula (expenditure approach) are the same. Changes in consumer confidence, fiscal policy, interest rates, and other factors influence shifts in AD.

On the other hand, the Aggregate Supply (AS) curve depicts the correlation between the price level and the quantity of goods that firms are willing to supply. The AS curve can exist in either the short run (SRAS) or the long run (LRAS), depending on the responsiveness of output to changes in the price level.

Multiplier Effect: The proportionate rise in ultimate revenue that follows a boost to spending is known as the multiplier effect.

Formula:

$$\text{Multiplier} = 1 \div (1 - MPC)$$

Where, MPC is Marginal Propensity to Consume.

This multiplier demonstrates how an initial change in spending can lead to a larger overall change in income and output.

Fiscal Policy: Budget Deficit and Surplus: Government spending and taxation decisions are what fiscal policy involves. When government spending exceeds revenue, a budget deficit occurs, and when revenue exceeds spending, a surplus occurs.

Formula for the Government Balanced Budget:

Balance Budget= T-G

Where

T = tax Revenue

G = Government Spending.

A positive balance indicates a surplus, while a negative balance indicates a deficit.

National Savings: The total savings in an economy, comprising both private and public savings, are known as national savings..

Formula:

National Savings = Private Savings + Public Savings.

Where:

Private savings are the income remaining after households pay their taxes and consume.

Public savings are the government's budget balance.

In a closed economy, national savings are equal to investment:

S = I

Behavioral Economics

With a view to better understand how human beings make choices within the actual global—wherein people are not always the logical actors that conventional economics considers them to Behavioral economics combines insights from psychology and economics. Behavioral economics recognizes that human conduct is impacted by biases, feelings, cognitive limits, and social impacts. This is in contrast to classical economic theory, which contends that human beings act to maximize price based on the best records and steady alternatives. This area of study aims to provide a more sophisticated understanding of decision-making processes by elucidating anomalies in economic models.

This region takes a look at pursuits to provide greater sophisticated expertise in decision-making processes by using elucidating anomalies in economic models.

The observation of ways psychological, emotional, cognitive, and social elements affect monetary decisions is referred to as behavioural economics. It differs from conventional economics in that it recognises that biases, a lack of cognitive capability, and environmental factors often reason humans to make choices that aren't rational.

The critique of the classical economic idea's rational agent version, or homo economicus, bureaucracy is the premise of behavioural economics. According to this conventional perspective, people are logical marketers who stabilise costs and benefits to reach satisfactory alternatives. This concept is challenged by behavioural economics, which shows that people generally use heuristics or intellectual shortcuts, are subject to cognitive biases, and are impacted by social norms, reciprocity, equity, and other issues.

The Significance of Behavioural Economics

Better Policy Design: The usage of behavioural economics in coverage-making is one of its major contributions. Governments and organizations create interventions, also known as "nudges," primarily based on expertise from this difficulty to help people make higher decisions without proscribing their freedom of preference. For instance, despite the fact that people can nonetheless choose out, making automated enrollment the default option in retirement financial savings plans has considerably raised participation costs.

Understanding Consumer Behavior: Businesses and marketers can advantage a more correct knowledge of client conduct by using behavioral economics. Greater green advertising processes, product designs, and pricing schemes can result from expertise in why people procrastinate, why they feel losses more than gains (loss aversion), or why they overvalue immediate advantages (hyperbolic discounting).

Addressing Economic Anomalies: Certain oddities, which include why humans purchase lottery tickets even when their possibilities of triumphing are slim or why they keep onto their depreciating equities (the endowment impact), defy the explanation provided by means of conventional financial fashions. A framework for analyzing those behaviors is furnished by behavioral economics, which facilitates to create better fashions that more closely fit the actual world.

Improving Financial Decision-Making: Making financial decisions, like making an investment, paying off debt, or preparing for retirement, can be tough for plenty of people. In line with behavioural economics, people might make the most of truthful treatments that take into consideration their mental propensities to put things off or give in to short-term temptations, such as automatic financial savings plans.

Enhanced Health Outcomes: Behavioural economics is used in the healthcare industry to inspire more healthy lifestyle selections. Applications that offer incentives for following prescription regimens or upholding a healthy lifestyle, for instance, use social contrast and on-the-spot rewards as a way of encouraging human beings to adjust their behaviour.

Scope

Decision-Making Under Uncertainty: Traditional economics means that humans compare risk and uncertainty logically and constantly. However, behavioural economics emphasises how heuristics and biases play a part in making choices in the face of uncertainty. Human beings regularly overestimate the opportunity of unusual but dramatic catastrophes, like airline crashes, whilst underestimating the probability of more common, but equally possible incidents, like vehicle accidents.

Time-Inconsistent Preferences: Behavioral economics examines how human beings' locate varying values on contemporary and future benefits. This is known as present bias or hyperbolic discounting, when people prioritize short-term profits above long-term advantages when making decisions. This has great effects on topics including budget addiction, and health-related practices.

Social Preferences and Fairness: Behavioral economics acknowledges that human beings care about justice and are stimulated through social options, in evaluation to standard monetary models that place an emphasis on self-interest. For instance, in tests like the Ultimatum sport, individuals usually reject offers they view as unjust, even at a price to themselves. These realizations are crucial for comprehending salary bargaining, social collaboration, and setting.

Market Behaviour: The study of behavioural economics additionally looks at how markets behave while players act irrationally. It looks at how herd mentality, overconfidence, and loss aversion can cause market inefficiencies, bubble bursts, and crashes. A department of behavioural economics known as "behavioural finance" researches these phenomena when it comes to monetary markets.

Behavioral Game Theory: This field uses game theory and psychological insights to recognize strategic interactions. Conventional game theory makes the supposition that contributors are logical and constantly try to maximize their profits. Alternatively, behavioral sport concept takes into consideration the possibility that contributors can be stricken by feelings, have constrained foresight, and feature finite rationality.

Nudging and Choice Architecture: Creating choice environments that influence behavior without proscribing freedom is one of the most beneficial uses of behavioural economics. "Nudges" are small modifications to the manner options are provided that have the power to significantly alter behaviour. Placing healthy meals at eye level, for example, can inspire customers to make better nutritional choices.

Features of the Behavioural Economics

Incorporation of Psychological Insights: Findings from psychology are integrated into behavioural economics, especially with regards to understanding how feelings, intellectual shortcuts, and cognitive biases have an effect on decision-making. Affirmation bias, availability bias, and the status quo bias are examples of cognitive biases that play a significant role in explaining why humans frequently make illogical choices.

Focus on Bounded Rationality: Conventional economics operates below the premise that humans possess countless cognitive capacities to understand facts and reach conclusions. Behavioral economics acknowledges that people possess limited rationality, which means they're limited in their potential to make selections by time, statistics, and mental capability, which forces them to depend upon heuristics and widespread pointers.

Emphasis on Social and Emotional Factors: The social environment of decision-making is taken under consideration by way of behavioural economics. Human beings' selections are frequently impacted by their emotional states, different human actions, and social requirements. For example, people may tip waitstaff even in conditions where they don't anticipate interacting with them again due to social conventions or feelings of guilt.

Non-Linear Preferences: Conventional economic models operate under the belief that possibilities are linear and stable across time. However, behavioural economics suggests that human choices are not linear. For instance, loss aversion, the tendency for humans to rate future losses more exceptionally than similar rewards, can result in threat-averse conduct even in conditions in which taking a hazard is more likely than not.

Experimental Approach: Behavioral economists use experiments a lot, typically in managed environments, to see how real humans act in specific conditions. Through systematically deviating from the expectancies of traditional financial idea, these experiments provide proof in favour of alternative human behaviour fashions.

Interdisciplinary Approach: Because it seeks to explain human behaviour more comprehensively, behavioural economics is intrinsically interdisciplinary, drawing on disciplines like psychology, neuroscience, sociology, and even anthropology. Because of its multidisciplinary nature, it's a flexible place with many applications in different fields.

Essential Ideas in Behavioral Economics

In order to describe how people make decisions in the actual world, behavioural economics consists of thoughts from psychology, which stress situations conventional monetary theories. In keeping with classical financial idea, humans are logical sellers that continually purpose to maximize their software. But behavioural economics recognizes that human selection-making is regularly illogical, impacted by the resource of social impacts, feelings, biases, and cognitive constraints. Behavioural economics is based on a few fundamental thoughts that explain why humans behave in ways that are not regular with classical economics and why they sometimes seem to make irrational choices.

Bounded Rationality: Bounded rationality is an essential idea inside the discipline of behavioural economics. Traditional economics makes the idea that humans can make logical selections because they have ideal statistics at their disposal and an endless supply of cognitive capability. Behavioural economics, however, acknowledges that humans have cognitive limits and frequently can't understand all relevant statistics at the same time whilst making judgments. As a result, humans start using intellectual shortcuts, or heuristics, to make decisions easier. These heuristics may be beneficial, but they can also result in less-than-perfect choices.

In contrast to maximizing, humans "satisfice," or search for a solution that is ideal enough rather than the best possible outcome, consistent with Herbert Simon, the Nobel laureate who first offered the concept of bounded rationality. This perception has full-size ramifications for economic models because it shows that human beings regularly make choices which might be pushed by means of cognitive constraints instead of ones that maximize price.

Heuristics and Biases: People utilize more than a few biases and heuristics (mental shortcuts) whilst making decisions, which behavioural economics has uncovered. Heuristics can help make tough judgments less difficult to deal with, however they can often bring about biases or systemic errors. Among the most well-known biases and heuristics are:

Availability Heuristic: People frequently use the convenience with which they are able to remember examples to estimate the opportunity of an event. For example, despite the fact that flying is normally more secure than riding, human beings might also overestimate the hazard of flying after reading about aircraft tragedies in the news.

Anchoring Bias: Anchoring is the tendency for human beings to base their choices unduly on the primary piece of records they're given, or the "anchor." as an example, if a supplier makes a high initial offer for a product, even if it is unreasonable, future discussions will often center on that high fee.

Confirmation Bias: people regularly search for, analyze, and retain records in a manner that helps their preconceived notions. Because of this prejudice, human beings may dismiss information that challenges their opinions, which may result in poor decision-making.

Framing Effect: Decisions can be greatly impacted with the aid of the manner data is offered. For instance, even though both statements offer the equal data, people are much more likely to pick out a scientific remedy if it is stated to have a 90% fulfillment rate rather than a 10% failure rate.

The conventional economics assumption of rationality is known as into question with the aid of these heuristics and biases. Behavioral economists are able to more appropriately forecast actual human conduct by comprehending how those intellectual shortcuts affect decision-making.

Prospect Theory and Loss Aversion: Daniel Kahneman and Amos Tversky created prospect theory, that is one of the maximum important ideas in behavioural economics. It contradicts the conventional utility hypothesis, which holds that people regard profits and losses on an identical footing. Rather, prospect theory indicates that human beings have a heightened sensitivity to losses in preference to benefits, a circumstance known as loss aversion.

Prospect theory holds that people do no longer evaluate possible opportunities in absolute phrases, but as an alternative when it comes to a reference point, generally their modern condition. Then, perceptions of profits and losses are altered, with losses appearing larger than profits. For example, it's also more painful to lose ₹1000 than it is to earn ₹1000. People may also become risk-averse in the case of winnings and risk-seeking in the case of losses as a result of this asymmetry in how they assess wins and losses.

Loss aversion provides an explanation for a number of real-world phenomena that are challenging to reconcile with classical economics. Examples include people's propensity to hang onto losing investments (in the hopes of avoiding realizing a loss) and their reluctance to switch from well-known products even in the face of superior alternatives.

Hyperbolic Discounting and Present Bias: The propensity for humans to favor smaller, immediate rewards over larger, delayed rewards is referred to as hyperbolic discounting, and it's a vital concept in behavioural economics. Present bias is the result of humans setting a disproportionate amount of weight on the present rather than the future. Conventional economics makes the assumption that people discount future benefits at a consistent rate, meaning that they might value ₹100 today more than ₹100 tomorrow, but that this rate of discounting future benefits does not change over time. However, behavioural economics clearly shows that people's preferences for different times are often inconsistent. When given the choice to get ₹100 now or ₹110 in a month, most consumers choose the immediate payout. However, individuals are more likely to choose the delayed incentive when given the option to choose between ₹100 in 12 months and ₹110 in 13 months. Hyperbolic discounting is confirmed by this contradiction.

Public policy, health behaviours, and monetary decision-making are all significantly impacted via present bias. It facilitates explaining why human beings often put matters off, forget to save for retirement, or partake in actions that fulfil their desires immediately but have destructive long-term outcomes, like smoking or overeating.

Endowment Effect: Another key idea in behavioral economics is the endowment effect. It alludes to the propensity for human beings to regard an item better simply due to the fact they own it. This goes against conventional financial ideas expectations, which state that an object's value should be determined by its ownership.

Experiments in which participants are given an object (e.g., a pen or mug) and requested how a whole lot they could be organized to sell it for can monitor the endowment effect. The fee they typically demand in change for the item is generally an awful lot greater than the price they would be prepared to pay in the event that they were not already in possession of the item. Humans generally tend to overvalue what they already have, which has sensible ramifications for client conduct, negotiations, and marketplace transactions.

Status Quo Bias: The inclination to keep things as they're rather than make changes, specifically whilst doing so may be high-quality, is referred to as reputation quo bias. Choice-making turns into inert when humans resist change and prefer the recognized. A mixture of loss aversion, the endowment impact, and the anxiety associated with creating a poor preference would possibly result in this bias.

Repute quo bias is particularly important with regards to customer selections, healthcare, and retirement budget. For example, because they are hesitant to change the repute quo, many people hold of their default retirement plans in place of selecting a probably better alternative. Insurance interventions that use inertia to boost savings behavior, like automated enrollment in retirement plans, were made possible by the aid of an understanding of this bias.

Social Preferences and Reciprocity: Behavioral economics recognizes the significance of social choices and reciprocity in decision-making, in comparison to classical economics, which holds that people behave for their own satisfactory hobbies. Fairness, equity, and the effect of one's moves on others are critical to human beings. They regularly have the willingness to forgo their very own monetary security to be able to reward or penalize just movement.

Studies together with the Dictator game and the Ultimatum game have verified that human nature isn't totally self-serving. One participant is granted cash in the Ultimatum game, and they need to provide some of it to another participant. Each player loses out if the second participant declines the offer. According to classical economics, the second player should accept any offer because something is better than nothing. In fact, however, people frequently turn down offers that they feel are unjust, even if it means losing out on something. This behaviour suggests a preference for reciprocity and justice.

Nudging and Choice Architecture: The idea of decision architecture and nudging is one of behavioural economics' most useful applications. Designing selection settings with a diffused approach has an impact on people's conduct without limiting their freedom of desire, which is referred to as nudging. This method acknowledges that even minor adjustments to the way options are presented could have a huge impact on how choices are made.

For example, although personnel are allowed to choose out, it has been confirmed that placing automatic enrollment as the default alternative in retirement savings plans will significantly increase participation fees. Further, cafeterias can inspire healthier ingesting conduct without proscribing the amount of junk food that customers can select by setting more healthy alternatives at eye degree.

The idea of nudging, which won a reputation from Richard Thaler and Cass Sunstein's eBook Nudge, has been used in many contexts, together with purchaser conduct, environmental upkeep, and public fitness. Policymakers and corporations can create interventions that help people make better decisions by utilizing insights from the behavioural economics sector.

To sum up, because behavioural economics takes into account psychological insights and acknowledges that human beings regularly break from rationality, it gives deeper information on human choice-making. Theories like prospect principle, loss aversion, heuristics and biases, and restricted rationality offer motives for humans's apparently illogical selections. Designing rules, advertising campaigns, making economic selections, and developing health solutions are all impacted by behavioural economics. Behavioural economics gives an extra useful and practical framework for comprehending how humans make decisions by thinking of the cognitive constraints, biases, and social effects on conduct.

Environmental Economics

A branch of economics referred to as "environmental economics" studies the financial implications of environmental problems. It investigates how herbal resources are used and dispensed, how financial activity influences the environment, and how rules can both save you from environmental deterioration and develop sustainable development. Environmental economics offers frameworks and contraptions to stabilise financial increases by addressing environmental issues such as pollution, deforestation, climate trade, and useful resource depletion. This is carried out by incorporating the surroundings into the selection-making procedure of the financial system.

The vicinity of economics that makes a speciality of the interaction between the environment and the economy is known as environmental economics. It aims to recognise the connection between economic interest and the surroundings, as well as the approaches wherein environmental policies may be advanced to ensure the sustainable and effective use of herbal resources. Economists contend that when environmental fees of manufacturing and consumption aren't absolutely represented in market expenses, market screw-ups frequently cause environmental concerns..

Scope:

Market Failures and Externalities: Resolving market imperfections, specifically externalities— situations in which the full fees or advantages of monetary hobby aren't absorbed by way of folks who provoke them—is one of the foremost goals of environmental economics. Pollution is a traditional example of a bad externality, wherein industries may also emit damaging emissions without struggling the whole value, whilst society at large suffers the outcomes. The purpose of environmental economics is to create laws in an effort to internalize these externalities and keep polluters chargeable for the damage they do to the environment.

Valuation of Environmental Goods and Services: Many of the commodities and services that the surroundings offer—like clean air, water, forests, and biodiversity—aren't exchanged in conventional markets and, as a end result, haven't any set price. Through creating techniques to calculate the economic well worth of these services and products, environmental economists help choice-makers in spotting the significance of conservation initiatives and allocating assets as a result.

Natural Resource Economics: Natural resource management, together with that of non-renewable assets like minerals and fossil fuels, as well as renewable resources like fisheries and forests, is another area of emphasis for environmental economics. The high extraction costs, trade-offs between immediate and future use, and the sustainable usage of these assets are all included.

Climate Change Economics: Climate change is a major environmental difficulty with full-size financial results. Environmental economics examines the charges and advantages of mitigating weather alteration, the monetary effects of climate change regulations, and the way to help the transition to a low – carbon economic system. It also explores the position of carbon pricing (including carbon taxes and cap-and-trade structures) in reducing carbon emissions.

Sustainable Development: Environmental economics is intently linked to the concept of sustainable improvement, which seeks to balance economic growth with environmental protection and social equity. It emphasizes the need to consider the long-term environmental effects of economic decisions and to ensure that future generations can meet their needs.

Applications of Environmental Economics

Pollution Control: Environmental economics gives policymakers with equipment to layout powerful pollution control measures. As an instance, many countries have carried out carbon pricing mechanisms, inclusive of carbon taxes and cap-and-trade structures, to lessen greenhouse gas emissions. These rules offer incentives for groups and individuals to adopt cleaner technology and reduce their environmental impact.

Renewable Energy Promotion: Environmental economists play an essential role in promoting the transition to renewable electricity sources. By means of studying the costs and benefits of renewable energy technologies, including solar, wind, and hydropower, they can help design policies, such as subsidies or feed-in tariffs, that encourage investment in clean energy.

Water Resource Management: Water is a vital natural resource, and its efficient allocation is a key problem in environmental economics. Economists expand models to optimize water use in agriculture, industry, and families even as ensuring that water sources are managed sustainably. Pricing mechanisms, consisting of water tariffs, can also be used to inspire conservation.

Biodiversity Conservation: Environmental economics helps to quantify the economic price of biodiversity and ecosystem offerings, which includes pollination, carbon sequestration, and water purification. This information is used to lay out regulations that protect biodiversity, including payment for ecosystem services

(PES) schemes, where landowners are compensated for retaining ecosystems.

Climate Change Mitigation and Adaptation: Environmental economics affords insights into the costs of weather change and the blessings of mitigation and model measures. It facilitates governments and global corporations' layout weather guidelines that stability the want for economic development with the urgency of decreasing emissions. Additionally, environmental economists investigate the economic impacts of climate change on inclined populations and sectors, such as agriculture, and advise strategies for building resilience.

Environmental Policy Design: Environmental economists work with governments and worldwide businesses to design and evaluate environmental policies. They use monetary modeling and empirical analysis to assess the effectiveness of different policy instruments, including taxes, subsidies, and regulations, in achieving environmental goals. For example, the European Union's Emissions Trading System (EU ETS) is a cap-and-trade system designed to reduce greenhouse gas emissions in the region.

Waste Management: Environmental economics contributes to the layout of efficient waste control structures, by analysing the fees and benefits of recycling, composting, and waste-to-energy technologies. Economists assist policymakers in broadening strategies to reduce waste generation and promote the circular economy.

Natural Disaster Risk Management: Environmental economists have a look at the monetary impact of natural screw-ups, including floods, hurricanes, and wildfires, and advise techniques for catastrophe risk reduction and management. They examine the costs of preparedness, response, and restoration measures and develop guidelines to enhance resilience to weather-associated dangers.

Essential Idea in Environmental Economics

Externalities: As stated earlier, externalities refer to the accidental consequences of financial activities that have an effect on 1/3 events. Poor externalities, together with pollution, impose costs on society, while high-quality externalities, which include conservation efforts, generate blessings. Environmental economics pursuits to accurately address those market disasters by way of internalizing externalities via coverage interventions.

Public Goods: Many environmental sources, together with easy air and biodiversity, are public goods which are probably non-excludable and non-rivalrous. This means no person may be excluded from the usage of them, and one person's use does not lessen their availability to others. But public goods are often subject to overuse and degradation, leading to the "tragedy of the commons." Environmental economists observe a way to manage public goods to prevent over-exploitation.

Property Rights: The task of belongings rights is a critical tool in environmental economics for dealing with natural assets. Actually, described and enforceable property rights can offer incentives for aid proprietors to use them sustainably. For instance, non-public possession of forests can inspire reforestation efforts and prevent deforestation.

Cost-Benefit Analysis: Environmental economists use Cost-Benefit Analysis (CBA) to evaluate the trade-offs among the expenses of environmental policies and the benefits they generate. CBA includes evaluating the economic costs of implementing a policy with the predicted environmental, health, and economic benefits. This method allows policymakers to make informed decisions about environmental interventions.

Pigovian Taxes: Named after economist Arthur Pigou, Pigovian taxes are designed to accurate bad externalities via enforcing a tax on sports that generate environmental damage. For example, a carbon tax places a rate on carbon emissions, encouraging corporations and people to reduce their carbon footprint.

Tradable Permits (Cap-and-Trade Systems): Tradable lets are some other market-based totally tools used to lessen pollutants. Beneath a cap-and-alternate system, a government sets a cap on trendy emissions, and problem permits that allow organisations to emit a tremendous quantity of pollution. Organisations can buy and sell lets in, growing a market for pollutants rights. This device provides flexibility for agencies to reduce emissions in a fee-powerful way.

Natural Capital: Natural capital refers to the inventory of natural resources and ecosystems that offer items and services important to human well-being. Environmental economics emphasizes the need to shield and enhance natural capital to ensure the sustainability of economic activities.

To sum up, environmental economics plays a critical role in addressing a number of the most urgent and demanding environmental situations of our time. Integrating financial ideas with environmental worries affords a framework for knowledge of the trade-offs between economic growth and environmental sustainability. The concepts of externalities, public goods, and herbal capital help policymakers design powerful interventions to accurate market failures and sell the green use of herbal resources. Through its applications in pollutant control, renewable energy advertising, climate change mitigation, and resource management, environmental economics offers practical answers for reaching a sustainable and resilient destiny. The field continues to evolve, adapting to new environmental challenges and contributing to the global effort to defend the planet even as fostering financial prosperity.

Political Economics

Political economics, or political economic system, is an interdisciplinary discipline that integrates economics, political, technological know-how, and sociology to take a look at how political forces have an effect on financial structures and, conversely, how financial systems affect political electricity. It lines its roots lower back to the classical economists like Adam Smith, David Ricardo, and Karl Marx, who recognized that the financial system can't be understood in isolation from political and social systems. Through the years, the scope of political economics has expanded, adapting to shifts within the worldwide political landscape and evolving economic theories.

These days, political economics is particularly relevant in studying the relationship between governments and markets, the distribution of wealth and sources, and the dynamics between the kingdom and personal corporation. It provides insights into how coverage decisions affect economic consequences, how political ideologies have an effect on monetary growth, and the way the interplay of establishments can both foster or inhibit monetary development. This introduction outlines the definition, scope, and various applications of political economics, underlining its importance as a framework for expertise in the complexities of contemporary political and economic systems.

Political economics can be extensively described because it takes a look at the ways political institutions, the political environment, and the economic machine—capitalist, socialist, or mixed—interact to shape financial regulations and effects. It includes know-how on how public policies are formulated, applied, and adjusted based on political manners, in addition to how economic strength may be used to influence political decisions.

One of the core standards of political economics is the recognition that financial choices are not made in a vacuum; they are encouraged by means of social, cultural, and political factors. Political economics acknowledges that policy alternatives—inclusive of taxation, law, public spending, or exchange rules—are often motivated by the pastimes of diverse stakeholders, together with politicians, hobby organizations, corporations, and citizens. In this manner, political economics extends beyond the narrow evaluation of markets and expenses, emphasizing the wider institutional and social elements that shape financial conduct.

Scope:

Public Policy and Governance: Political economics plays an important role in the knowledge of how governments formulate policies. This includes guidelines on taxation, welfare, environmental regulations, and exertions markets. Political economists look at how these rules are fashioned by means of political events, interest corporations, and public opinion.

Monetary structures: exceptional political structures supply upward thrust to extraordinary financial results. Political economics examines the consequences of capitalism, socialism, and mixed economies, comparing their strategies to useful resource allocation, wealth distribution, and economic growth. It analyzes how the political weather in a rustic affects its economic system, such as the role of important planning in socialist economies or the influence of unfastened markets in capitalist structures.

International Political financial system: Political economics additionally has a global measurement. It deals with international alternate, foreign policy, and international governance institutions like the World Trade Organization (WTO) and International Monetary Fund (IMF). It examines how globalization, change agreements, and international rules affect countrywide economies and the way political conflicts—inclusive of change wars—form worldwide markets.

Development Economics: Political economics is vital in information on the development procedure of countries. It researches how institutions, governance structures, and political balance or instability impact economic growth, poverty, and inequality in developing international locations. Political economists pay attention to how political elements—like corruption, dictatorship, or democratic governance—have an effect on economic development and the effectiveness of policy interventions.

Welfare Economics and Social Justice: Another vital factor of political economics is its problem with the distribution of wealth and resources. Political economists analyze how policies related to welfare, fitness care, schooling, and housing are stimulated via political elements and how these policies have an effect on social justice and inequality.

Environmental Economics: As environmental troubles end up more pressing, political economics examines the political and economic factors influencing environmental coverage. It considers how governments stability financial growth with sustainability and how political pressures affect selections on climate trade, strength guidelines, and natural resource management.

Behavioral Political Financial System: This branch focuses on the interaction between political institutions and human behaviour. It incorporates insights from psychology and sociology to understand how political biases, ideologies, and collective behaviour influence economic decision-making. This is particularly relevant in understanding voting behaviour, public opinion, and the role of identity politics in shaping economic policies.

Applications of Political Economics

Formulating monetary policies: One of the primary applications of political economics is inside the components of public regulations. Governments use political economic evaluation to layout regulations that balance economic performance with political feasibility. For example, the creation of a progressive taxation system may be driven by the need to reduce inequality, but it also needs to be politically acceptable to different interest groups.

Know-how Political have an impact on Markets: Political economics allows in analysing how political moves affect markets. For example, government regulations, changes in price lists, and subsidies can considerably impact market expenses, competitiveness, and market access. Political economists assist in understanding how these interventions have an effect on industries, markets, and economies.

Evaluating the impact of Political systems: Political economics allows for the evaluation of how different political structures—democracies, autocracies, and hybrids—have an effect on monetary performance. For example, democratic structures may additionally set regulations that are more inclusive but also pose challenges to inefficiencies like lobbying and vote buying. Autocracies might promote rapid growth in the short term but at the cost of long-term sustainability and equity.

Global relations and exchange policy: Political economics plays an essential role in analysing global exchange agreements, sanctions, and trade wars. For instance, political economists might evaluate how tariffs imposed during a trade war impact domestic industries, global relations, and international supply chains. This is essential for understanding the interplay between national interests and international economic interdependence.

Electoral Economics: Political economists look at how financial situations have an effect on elections and political balance. For instance, high unemployment rates, inflation, or recessions can lead to political instability, influencing electoral outcomes. In turn, politicians regularly base their election campaigns on monetary promises, using political economic analysis to craft strategies that appeal to voters.

Inequality and Redistribution: Political economics is central to debates on inequality and redistribution. Governments use insights from political economics to design welfare programs, social safety systems, and public healthcare. These policies are shaped by political ideologies—left-wing parties may desire more redistributive rules, while right-wing parties may focus on market-based solutions.

Policy suggestions for improvement: In developing countries, political economics is used to design policies that promote economic growth, reduce poverty, and improve governance. Political economists provide insights on how political instability, corruption, and weak institutions preclude development, offering guidelines on reforms that could stabilize political conditions and promote inclusive growth.

Environmental Coverage and Sustainability: Political economics also has vital packages in environmental economics. Governments use political economic analysis to design rules geared toward decreasing carbon emissions, holding assets, and promoting sustainable improvement. The interaction among political pursuits and environmental desires is a key vicinity of research for political economists, especially within the context of weather exchange negotiations and global environmental agreements.

Public Choice Theory: Public desire idea is a subfield of political economics that applies financial analysis to political choice-making. It assumes that politicians, voters, and bureaucrats act in their very own self-interest, and it seeks to provide an explanation for how those hobbies shape public coverage. This theory has essential applications in understanding issues like rent-seeking, corruption, and inefficiencies in government.

Disaster management and monetary balance: Political economics also applies to the control of monetary crises, along with recessions, financial crises, or pandemics. Political economists examine how governments respond to crises, the political pressures they face, and the long-term monetary results in their decisions. For instance, the 2008 monetary disaster prompted political economic debates at the function of government in regulating economic markets and imparting bailouts.

Essential Idea in Political Economics

Public Choice Theory: Public Choice Theory is one of the foundational concepts in political economics. It applies economic reasoning to the behaviour of political actors, including politicians, bureaucrats, and voters. The core assumption is that political agents, like individuals in the market, act in their self-interest. This theory challenges the notion that politicians and public officials naturally work for the public good. Instead, it posits that they are motivated by personal goals such as power, influence, and wealth.

The theory also addresses how political decisions are made and the inefficiencies that arise from the self-interested behaviour of politicians. For example, politicians might implement policies that favour special interest groups (who offer political support or financial backing) rather than the general population. This leads to government failure, just as market failure occurs when individual actors in the marketplace make decisions that lead to inefficiencies or inequities.

Implications of Public Choice Theory: Government inefficiency: Bureaucrats and politicians might favour policies that benefit themselves or small, powerful interest groups, leading to outcomes that may not be optimal for society.

Rent-seeking behaviour: This occurs when individuals or groups use political influence to obtain economic gains without contributing to productivity. Rent-seeking can distort market outcomes, lead to corruption, and increase inequality.

Voting paradoxes: Public Choice Theory also examines collective decision-making and the potential for irrational outcomes in democratic systems. The preferences of the majority may not align with the optimal policy for the broader economy.

Rent-Seeking and Political Power: Rent-seeking is a central concept in political economics and refers to the pursuit of economic rents through manipulation of the political environment rather than through productive economic activities. Economic rent refers to any excess payment made to a factor of production (land, labour, or capital) over its opportunity cost.

In political terms, rent-seeking involves lobbying or using political influence to secure benefits such as government subsidies, tariffs, favourable regulations, or monopoly rights. These benefits often come at the expense of broader economic efficiency, as resources are allocated based on political power rather than market demand.

Examples of Rent-Seeking:

A company lobbying the government for a monopoly in a particular industry.

Seeking tax exemptions or favourable regulations that give one group an advantage over competitors.

Rent-seeking can have detrimental effects on the economy by distorting market outcomes, increasing inequality, and fostering corruption. Political power, rather than economic efficiency, becomes the primary driver of resource allocation.

Institutional Economics: Institutional economics is a critical subfield within political economics that focuses on the role of institutions—

formal laws, regulations, informal social norms, and conventions—in shaping economic behavior. Institutions are seen as the "rules of the game" that govern the interactions between individuals and organizations in a society.

Douglass North, a key figure in this field, emphasised that institutions shape the incentives and constraints faced by economic actors. Effective institutions create a stable environment for economic transactions by reducing uncertainty and promoting trust. For instance, well-functioning legal systems protect property rights, enforce contracts, and regulate markets, fostering economic growth. In contrast, weak institutions (e.g., corruption, lack of legal enforcement) hinder economic development and can lead to poverty traps.

Key Insights from Institutional Economics:

Path dependency: Institutional development follows a path-dependent process, meaning that historical events and decisions shape current institutional structures, often making reform difficult.

Formal vs. informal institutions: Both formal laws and informal social norms play crucial roles in shaping economic outcomes. Informal norms can sometimes override formal institutions, especially in contexts with weak governance.

The State vs. Market Debate: The relationship between the state and the market is a longstanding debate in political economics. This debate centres on the role of the government in regulating economic activity and managing the distribution of resources. There are two opposing schools of thought:

Free market advocates: Economists like Adam Smith and Milton Friedman argue that markets should be left to operate with minimal government intervention. They believe that individuals acting in their own self-interest will naturally lead to efficient outcomes through the "invisible hand" of the market.

State interventionists: Thinkers like John Maynard Keynes argue that markets are prone to failures, such as monopolies, externalities, and business cycles. Therefore, government intervention is necessary to correct these failures, maintain economic stability, and ensure a fair distribution of resources.

This debate continues to shape economic policy across the globe. Neoliberal policies (promoting deregulation, privatization, and reduced state intervention) contrast with more interventionist approaches that advocate for government involvement in managing economic inequality, providing social safety nets, and regulating industries to prevent market failures.

Political Business Cycle: The political business cycle theory suggests that politicians, particularly in democratic systems, may manipulate the economy to improve their chances of being re-elected. This theory posits that governments may engage in expansionary fiscal or monetary policies before elections to boost economic activity, create jobs, and improve public sentiment.

Such short-term policies can lead to inflation or long-term economic instability once the election is over. Political business cycles demonstrate how political motives can sometimes lead to suboptimal economic outcomes, driven by the desire for electoral success rather than sound economic management.

Examples: Governments cutting taxes or increasing public spending before an election to stimulate the economy, even if it results in long-term fiscal imbalances.

Central banks potentially delaying interest rate hikes to avoid harming economic growth during an election cycle.

Globalization and International Political Economy: Political economics also studies the effects of globalization and how international economic policies are shaped by political forces. Globalization involves the increased interconnectedness of countries through trade, investment, and finance. Political economists study how political factors—such as national interests, power dynamics, and global institutions—affect global trade agreements, monetary policies, and international relations.

International institutions like the World Trade Organization (WTO), International Monetary Fund (IMF) and World Bank play a significant role in shaping the rules of global trade and finance. However, political conflicts between nations, such as trade wars or geopolitical tensions, can significantly disrupt global markets and economic cooperation.

Inequality and Redistribution: Economic inequality is a major concern in political economics. The distribution of wealth and income is often shaped by political decisions, and the level of inequality within a society can influence political stability. Governments use tools like taxation, welfare programs, and public services to redistribute resources and address inequality.

Political economists examine the trade-offs between economic efficiency and equity. For example, progressive taxation (where higher-income individuals pay a larger percentage of their income in taxes) may reduce inequality but could also discourage investment and productivity if not carefully designed.

The political feasibility of redistributive policies often depends on the balance of power between different social groups. Wealthy elites may resist policies that threaten their economic position, while disadvantaged groups may push for more redistributive measures.

Behavioral Political Economy: Behavioral political economy integrates insights from psychology into the study of political and economic decision-making. It challenges the traditional assumption that individuals always act rationally in their self-interest. Instead, it recognises that cognitive biases, emotions, and social factors often influence political and economic behaviour.

For example, voters may support policies that are against their economic interests due to emotional appeals, ideological commitment, or misinformation. Politicians, similarly, may make decisions based on short-term political gains rather than long-term economic benefits.

Collective Action Problem: The collective action problem is a key concept in understanding why groups with shared interests often fail to coordinate effectively. It explains why individuals may choose not to participate in collective efforts, such as voting or lobbying for public goods, even though they would benefit from the outcomes.

The free-rider problem is a specific manifestation of this issue: individuals may benefit from a public good (like clean air or public infrastructure) without contributing to its provision. In political economics, collective action problems are relevant to understanding why certain policies, like environmental regulations, are difficult to implement.

Regulation and Deregulation: Governments often regulate markets to correct market failures, such as monopolies, negative externalities (e.g., pollution), and information asymmetries. However, the extent and nature of regulation can vary widely depending on political ideology and economic conditions.

Deregulation refers to the reduction or elimination of government controls in an industry. Neoliberal economists argue that deregulation can promote competition, innovation, and economic efficiency. However, critics warn that excessive deregulation can lead to market failures, financial crises, or environmental degradation.

Evolution of Economics

Ancient Economic Theories

Ancient economic ideas became rooted within the practices and philosophies of early civilizations, which did not have formalized financial structures but engaged in activities including trade, taxation, and aid allocation. These early thoughts laid the foundation for later monetary theories and standards, influencing thinkers from the Classical generation through the Middle Ages and beyond. Ancient economists, or rather philosophers with economic thoughts, were generally concerned with questions of justice, ethics, wealth, poverty, and the distribution of resources. Many of their thoughts nevertheless resonate today, influencing cutting-edge debates on economic justice, political economy, and societal well-being.

This essay will explore the thoughts of ancient economic thinkers from the Mesopotamian, Greek, Roman, and early Chinese civilizations. We will look at key figures like Aristotle, Plato, Xenophon, and Chanakya, as well as touch upon the broader economic concepts of their respective cultures.

Economic notion in Early Mesopotamia and Egypt:

Historic Mesopotamia and Egypt had been some of the earliest known civilizations, and their economies were predominantly based on agriculture, trade, and state-controlled distribution. While there are no named "economists" from these periods, the economic practices of these civilizations were advanced and influenced later economic thought.

Mesopotamia:

The Sumerians, Babylonians, and Assyrians in Mesopotamia advanced sophisticated economies with complicated systems of trade, property rights, and taxation. The economy was normally agrarian, however, the location's fertile land and proximity to main rivers like the Tigris and Euphrates enabled surplus production, which became traded throughout lengthy distances.

Key monetary Practices: Temple and Palace Economies: In early Mesopotamia, the temple and palace had been the significant monetary establishments. They controlled significant tracts of land, controlled agricultural production, and gathered taxes. Surpluses were redistributed to the populace, mainly all through instances of famine or shortage.

Assets Rights and Contracts: The famous Code of Hammurabi (circa 1750 BCE) affords insight into the financial idea of the time. It info legal guidelines approximately assets, exchange, and labor relations, establishing clear policies for contracts, debt, interest, and wages. This codification of financial principles highlights the significance of regulating economic activities to ensure equity and stability.

Egypt:

In ancient Egypt, the economy became additionally state-managed, with the pharaoh acting as the pinnacle of both political and economic life. Like Mesopotamia, Egypt's economy was focused on agriculture, however, trade with neighboring regions (including Nubia and the Levant) was important for obtaining goods that were not available locally.

Key monetary Practices: Redistributive economy: The Egyptian state collected taxes in the form of grain, livestock, and other items. These resources were redistributed to the population through public works initiatives, including Bing the construction of temples and pyramids, and during periods of food shortage.

Barter system and exchange: Although a barter system was mainly used in internal trade, Egypt also engaged in foreign trade using precious metals. Trade routes extended into Africa, the Middle East, and the Mediterranean, bringing in luxury goods and resources like gold, timber, and incense.

Greek Monetary Notion: Plato, Aristotle, and Xenophon

Greek philosophers laid the inspiration for Western economic ideas, with discussions on the character of wealth, trade, and the function of the nation in monetary existence. Even as they did not address economics as a separate area, their philosophical inquiries into justice, society, and governance have monetary implications.

Plato (428–348 BCE)

Plato's monetary ideas are embedded in his broader philosophical works, especially The Republic and The Legal Guidelines. He became much less involved with the mechanics of economic structures and was more focused on the ethical dimensions of wealth and property.

Key economic Theories of Plato: Department of Hard Work: Plato mentioned the Department of Labor in the Republic, in which he argued that people should specialize in the duties for which they're quality proper. This concept is based on the principle that specialization ends in improved productivity and efficiency. Despite the fact that Plato's imagination and prescient ideas were tied to his ideal society, this early belief in the department of hard work is foundational to later economic ideas.

Communal assets and Guardians: In The Republic, Plato proposed that the ruling elegance (the "Guardians") ought to no longer have personal belongings. He believed that private ownership of wealth might corrupt rulers and result in injustice. As a substitute, the property needs to be held in commonplace to save you conflicts of hobby and make certain that rulers work for the not unusual accuracy.

Critique of commerce: Plato had a quite negative view of exchange and trade, associating them with greed and the erosion of civic virtue. He believed that immoderate pursuit of wealth could lead to moral decay and distract people from higher intellectual and moral hobbies.

Aristotle (384–322 BCE)

Aristotle, a scholar of Plato, presented a greater special and pragmatic method to economic problems. His writings, especially in Politics and Nicomachean Ethics, cope with the nature of wealth, assets, and exchange, supplying a foundational angle on economic family members.

Key economic Theories of Aristotle: Personal belongings: unlike Plato, Aristotle supported private property. He argued that non-public possession became natural and beneficial because it recommended people to paint more difficult and take higher care of their possessions. Aristotle believed that property possession was essential for private freedom and the pursuit of happiness.

The distinction between natural and Unnatural Acquisition: Aristotle is prominent among sorts of wealth acquisition. Natural acquisition worries about acquiring goods essential for survival and a terrific lifestyle (including meals and refuge), the time unnatural acquisition worries the accumulation of wealth for its personal sake, in particular through trade and money-lending. Aristotle criticized the latter, viewing it as morally suspect.

Exchange and money: Aristotle provided one of the earliest discussions of cash as a medium of change. He recognized that money emerged from the need to facilitate trade, as bartering was inefficient. He additionally introduced the concept of simple price, arguing that items must be exchanged at a charge that displays their authentic cost, selling fairness in exchange.

Xenophon (431–354 BCE)

Xenophon, a scholar of Socrates, became one of the first Greek thinkers to jot down appreciably about realistic monetary topics. His works, especially Oeconomicus and approaches and means, offer insights into the control of households, estates, and the economy of Athens.

Key financial Theories of Xenophon: Household control (Oikonomia): In Oeconomicus, Xenophon discussed the management of the family (oikos), which he saw as the fundamental unit of financial existence. He emphasized the importance of careful planning, budgeting, and the green use of resources to ensure prosperity.

Public Finance and revenue: In methods and approach, Xenophon provided practical recommendations for increasing the revenues of the Athenian country. He recommended reforms to enhance public finance, such as growing silver mining, promoting exchange, and inspiring overseas traders to settle in Athens. This work reflects his information of the importance of public coverage in dealing with the economic system.

Agriculture and Self-Sufficiency: Xenophon believed that agriculture was the most crucial monetary interest, as it supplied the necessary goods for survival and was seen as morally superior to exchange or cash-lending. He advocated for self-sufficiency and argued that the kingdom should sell agricultural improvement to ensure monetary stability.

Roman financial concept

Roman financial idea was pragmatic and focused on the realistic management of the empire's huge assets. The Romans were professional directors, and their economic rules were geared towards preserving the stability and prosperity of the empire. Key areas of Roman economic activity included agriculture, taxation, trade, and public works.

Key Figures in Roman economic concept: Cato the Elder (234–149 BCE): In his work De Agri Cultura, Cato the Elder emphasized the importance of agriculture as the muse of the Roman economy. He provided practical advice on property management, crop rotation, and livestock rearing. Cato believed that land possession and farming were the pillars of Roman monetary and social existence.

Cicero (106–43 BCE): Cicero, the Roman statesman and logician, touched on economic problems in his writings on ethics and politics. In De Officiis (On duties), Cicero mentioned the ethical implications of wealth and commerce. He believed that honest exchange was ideal, but he condemned profiteering and usury, viewing them as harmful to society.

Seneca (4 BCE–65 CE): The Stoic logician Seneca wrote considerably on wealth, poverty, and the ethical use of cash. In his letters and essays, Seneca argued that wealth should be used for the common good and that immoderate attachment to wealth was detrimental to personal virtue and societal well-being. He emphasized the importance of simplicity, self-restraint, and generosity.

Roman financial Practices:

Public Works and Infrastructure: The Romans invested heavily in public works, such as roads, aqueducts, and ports, which facilitated trade and advanced economic performance. These infrastructure tasks were funded by taxes and the spoils of conflict, reflecting the Roman nation's role in dealing with the economy.

Taxation and Tribute: The Roman Empire relied on a complex system of taxation and tribute to finance its army and administrative expenses. Taxes were levied on land, trade, and properties, while conquered territories were required to pay tribute to Rome. This system allowed the empire to extract wealth from its provinces while maintaining economic stability.

Historical Chinese monetary thought: Confucius and Legalism

Historical Chinese financial notion was shaped by Confucianism, Legalism, and Daoism. These philosophies encouraged the improvement of Chinese financial practices, especially in terms of governance, agriculture, and the role of the kingdom.

Confucius (551–479 BCE)

Confucius, the famous Chinese truth seeker, did now not write extensively about financial matters. However, his ideas on governance, social concord, and ethics had important implications for financial lifestyles in historical China. His teachings, accumulated in the Analects, pressured the importance of morality, social order, and the well-being of the people, which prolonged the realm of monetary control.

Key financial ideas of Confucius: Ethical, economic system and Governance: Confucius emphasized that rulers ought to govern with distinctive features and benevolence, prioritizing the welfare of their subjects. In terms of monetary idea, this intended that rulers must ensure that humans had enough resources to live readily, keeping off immoderate taxation or exploitation. A well-ruled state might result in prosperity because humans might be influenced to work hard and make contributions to the financial system in the event that they were handled justly.

Agriculture as the Inspiration for Wealth: Like many historical thinkers, Confucius believed that agriculture had changed into the most important financial hobby. He advocated for guidelines that supported farmers and ensured agricultural productivity. In his view, a stable and wealthy society trusted a sturdy agricultural base, and the nation should encourage farming whilst keeping off oppressive taxes on the agricultural area.

Social Concord and Wealth Distribution: Confucianism emphasized social concord and the proper relationships between one-of-a-kind members of society. Confucius believed that severe wealth and poverty brought about social discord and unrest. Consequently, while he no longer recommended strict equality, he believed that rulers needed to ensure a fair distribution of wealth to save social divisions and hold harmony.

Legalism and the economic system

In contrast to Confucianism, Legalism become a greater authoritarian and pragmatic philosophy that had a significant impact on Chineselanguage economic coverage at some point of the Qin Dynasty (221–206 BCE). Legalists believed withinthe strict enforcement of legal guidelines and centralized manage of the economic system to ensure the strength and stability of the nation.

Key financial thoughts of Legalism:

Country management of sources: Legalists believed that the state should have direct management over the economy to ensure that it may mobilize resources efficiently, specifically for military functions. This protected controlling agricultural manufacturing, taxation, and exchange. Legalists noticed the economy as a device for strengthening the kingdom, and they had been less concerned with the well-being of the character than with the energy of the kingdom.

Rewards and Punishments: Legalist economic policies were based on the principle of rewards and punishments. Farmers and workers who were productive were rewarded, while those who were not were punished. This strict system of incentives was designed to maximise economic output and ensure that the state had the resources it needed.

Standardization: The Legalist ruler Qin Shi Huang is famous for his efforts to standardize the Chinese economy, including the unification of weights and measures, currency, and writing systems. These reforms were aimed at facilitating trade and economic integration across the newly unified Chinese empire, making it easier for the state to control economic activities.

Chanakya (c. 350–283 BCE) and the Arthashastra

Chanakya, also known as Kautilya or Vishnugupta, was an ancient Indian philosopher, economist, and statesman who served as an advisor to the first Mauryan emperor, Chandragupta Maurya. His most famous work, the Arthashastra, is a treatise on statecraft, politics, and economics, offering one of the most comprehensive discussions of economic management in ancient times.

Key Economic Theories of Chanakya:

Role of the State in the Economy: The Arthashastra is a highly pragmatic text that advocates for the state to play a central role in managing the economy. Chanakya believed that the prosperity of the state depended on its ability to control resources, regulate trade, and ensure the security of its borders. The text outlines various ways in which the state can intervene in the economy to promote growth and stability, including land reforms, taxation policies, and public investment in infrastructure.

Taxation and Public Revenue: Chanakya emphasised the importance of taxation as the primary source of revenue for the state. However, he cautioned against excessive taxation, warning that it could lead to rebellion and reduce the overall wealth of the state. He proposed a balanced taxation system that would allow the state to fund its activities while encouraging economic productivity. The Arthashastra also details various types of taxes, including land taxes, trade taxes, and taxes on manufactured goods.

Agriculture and Trade: Like other ancient thinkers, Chanakya viewed agriculture as the backbone of the economy. He advocated for state policies that would promote agricultural development, including land reclamation, irrigation projects, and support for farmers. In addition to agriculture, Chanakya recognised the importance of trade, both domestic and international, as a source of wealth. The Arthashastra contains detailed advice on managing trade routes, regulating markets, and promoting commerce.

Welfare and Economic Justice: Although the Arthashastra is often seen as a Machiavellian text focused on power and control, it also contains elements of economic justice. Chanakya believed that a ruler's primary duty was to ensure the well-being of his subjects. He advocated for policies that would prevent extreme poverty and protect the most vulnerable members of society. For example, the state was responsible for providing relief in times of famine and ensuring that wealth was distributed in a way that did not lead to social unrest.

Economic Thought in Ancient Israel and the Hebrew Bible

The Hebrew Bible (Tanakh) contains numerous references to economic practices and principles, offering insight into the economic life of ancient Israel. While the Bible is primarily a religious and ethical text, it addresses issues of property, debt, justice, and charity, which have economic implications.

Key Economic Themes in the Hebrew Bible:

Sabbath and Jubilee Laws: The Torah contains specific laws related to the economy, such as the Sabbath and Jubilee years. Every seventh year, land was to lie fallow (the Sabbatical year), and every fiftieth year, all land was to be returned to its original owners (the Jubilee year). These laws were designed to prevent the concentration of wealth and land in the hands of a few and to provide economic relief for the poor and indebted. The Jubilee laws, in particular, reflect an ancient concern with economic justice and the redistribution of wealth.

Usury and Debt Forgiveness: The Hebrew Bible contains strict prohibitions against charging interest (usury) on loans to fellow Israelites. Loans were seen as a form of charity, not a business transaction, and were intended to help those in need. Additionally, debts were to be forgiven every seven years, providing a form of economic relief for the poor and preventing long-term debt bondage.

Justice and Charity: The Hebrew prophets frequently condemned economic injustice, particularly the exploitation of the poor by the wealthy. They called for fairness in trade, honest weights and measures, and the protection of vulnerable groups such as widows, orphans, and foreigners. The biblical concept of tzedakah (justice or righteousness) included acts of charity and support for those in need, emphasising that economic justice was a moral imperative.

Islamic School of Economic Thought

The Islamic school of Economic Thought is rooted in the concepts of Shariah (Islamic law) and gives a wonderful attitude on economics, specializing in ethics, justice, and the welfare of the community. At its core, Islamic economics revolves around key standards: the prohibition of usury (riba) and the merchandising of risk-sharing. In comparison to conventional finance, in which interest-based lending is commonplace, Islamic finance encourages profit-and-loss sharing via partnerships (such as mudarabah or musharakah), ensuring that wealth generation is a shared enterprise. This discourages exploitative practices and aligns with the Islamic ideal of monetary justice.

Wealth distribution is another vital characteristic. Islam promotes a balanced approach, in which excessive wealth accumulation is discouraged, and mechanisms such as zakat (a mandatory charity) ensure that wealth circulates within society. This redistribution system fosters harmony and decreases inequality, creating a safety net for the poor and underprivileged.

Moreover, Islamic economics prioritizes the ethical dimensions of economic activities. Companies are expected to function in a way that benefits society and avoids harm, adhering to principles of honesty, transparency, and fairness. Certain industries, such as alcohol, gambling, and meat production, are prohibited as they are considered harmful to individuals and society.

The overarching goal of the Islamic financial system is to promote social justice and welfare. It seeks a middle path between capitalism and socialism, avoiding the extremes of individualism and collectivism. By embedding ethical and moral values within its framework, Islamic economics offers an alternative model that emphasizes human welfare and equitable distribution of resources.

To sum up, Ancient economic thought was deeply intertwined with the social, political, and ethical concerns of early civilizations. While ancient thinkers did not develop formal economic theories in the modern sense, their ideas on property, wealth, trade, and governance laid the foundation for later economic thinking. The ancient world's focus on agriculture, the role of the state, and the ethical dimensions of wealth and poverty continues to influence contemporary economic debates. From the temple economies of Mesopotamia and Egypt to the philosophical inquiries of the Greeks and the practical wisdom of Chanakya and Confucius, ancient economic thought provides valuable insights into the fundamental questions of how societies manage resources and ensure the well-being of their people.

Classical Economist

Classical economics is one of the most influential schools of thought in economic theory, having laid the foundation for much of modern economics. It originated in the late 18th and early 19th centuries during the Enlightenment period, where thinkers and philosophers began to view economics as an awesome area of understanding. The main figures in classical economics include Adam Smith, David Ricardo, Thomas Malthus, Jean-Baptiste Say, and John Stuart Mill. This school of thought revolves around several key principles, including the belief in free markets, minimal government intervention, the importance of individual self-interest, and the idea that economies are self-regulating.

Adam Smith (1723–1790)

Adam Smith is regularly known as the "father of economics." His most splendid work, The Wealth of Nations (1776), is considered the foundational text of classical economics. Smith's theories are grounded in the idea that individuals act in their self-interest, and through this pursuit of personal gain, they contribute to the general good of society. His principle of the "invisible hand" suggests that people seeking to maximise their personal welfare inadvertently help to allocate resources in a way that benefits society as a whole.

Key Theories of Adam Smith:

The Invisible Hand: Smith's invisible hand concept is a metaphor for the self-regulating nature of markets. Consistent with this concept, when individuals act in their personal self-interest, markets tend to allocate assets efficiently. For example, a baker makes bread not because of a sense of charity, but because they want to earn a living. However, by producing bread, they meet a social need. In this way, the baker's self-interest aligns with the needs of society.

Division of Labour: Smith also underlined the significance of this concept. He maintained that as employees specialise in particular jobs, productivity rises. His well-known example of a pin factory, where each employee concentrates on a single step of the production process to increase efficiency, is frequently used to demonstrate this point. According to Smith, specialization promotes economic progress by enabling higher output.

Laissez-faire: Smith supported little government involvement in the business sector. He thought that markets function best when they are allowed to run unhindered by overbearing regulations or intrusive government intervention. He did acknowledge, however, that national defence, the preservation of property rights, and the provision of public goods like infrastructure are among the essential roles of government.

David Ricardo (1772–1823)

Another important thinker in classical economics was David Ricardo, who is most remembered for his theories on income distribution and international trade. *Principles of Political Economy and Taxation* (1817), his most important work, is where he offered various new concepts and developed Smith's views.

Key Theories of David Ricardo:

Comparative Advantage: Although they can produce everything more efficiently than other nations, governments should specialize in the production of the products they can produce most efficiently, according to Ricardo's thesis of comparative advantage, which has made him most famous. They can trade with other nations in order to increase economic welfare generally by doing this. The basis for contemporary ideas of international trade was established by this notion.

Ricardo gave the examples of Portugal and England to demonstrate this. He contended that Portugal was more efficient at producing wine, but England was more efficient at making fabric. Portugal and England would gain if Portugal focused on wine production and England on fabric production, trading with each other to acquire both items, even if Portugal could produce both goods more effectively than England.

Theory of Rent: Another significant addition to classical economics is Ricardo's Theory of rent. He maintained that the variation in land productivity determines rent. This hypothesis states that better-located or more productive land is worth more money. The gap between the productivity of a certain plot of land and the least productive land currently in use determines how much rent is paid. The rent on more productive land rises as the population develops and less fertile land is put under cultivation.

Labor Theory of Value: According to this theory, the amount of labour needed to make a good determines its value, and Ricardo shared this belief with Smith. But Ricardo improved on this notion by realising that labour is not always equally productive and that capital and the process of production can have an impact on a good's worth.

Thomas Malthus (1766–1834)

The main characteristic of Thomas Malthus is his pessimism regarding population growth and how it affects economic progress. An Essay on the Principle of Population (1798), his most important work, popularised the theory that widespread poverty and famine may result from population increase exceeding food production.

Key Theories of Thomas Malthus:

Malthusian Population Theory: According to Malthus, food production grows arithmetically (i.e., linearly) whereas population grows geometrically, doubling every 25 years under ideal conditions. Consequently, population growth would eventually outpace the economy's ability to generate food, creating a scenario in which war, disease, and starvation would drive the population back to levels that could support itself. It was dubbed the "Malthusian trap."

Malthus thought that as more people competed for fewer resources, unregulated population expansion would result in a drop in living standards. Because of his beliefs, he supported population control strategies including delaying marriage and exercising moral constraints to have fewer children.

Theory of Gluts: The concept that an economy may generate more things than it can consume is known as a general glut, and Malthus contributed to this discussion. He maintained that times of economic stagnation could result from high savings and low demand.

Jean-Baptiste Say (1767–1832)

French economist Jean-Baptiste Say is renowned for having developed "Say's Law," which has become a part of traditional economics. Even though Say expanded on Adam Smith's theories, there were several notable differences in his work, especially with regard to his theories of supply and demand.

Key Theories of Jean-Baptiste Say:

Say's Law of Markets: Say is most famous for having established Say's Law, which holds that "supply creates its own demand." Stated differently, the process of creating products and services brings in the money required to buy more goods and services. Say maintained that since the production of things generates an equal demand for them, there could never be a general oversupply of products in the economy. Say contends that those who produce items get paid, and they spend that money to buy more goods. This guarantees that there are no long-term shortages or surpluses in the economy and that it stays in equilibrium. Say's Law served as the foundation for the traditional view that markets are self-regulating and served as a key component of their case against government involvement in the economy.

John Stuart Mill (1806–1873)

One of the last great classical economists, John Stuart Mill's contributions signalled the shift from classical to neoclassical economics. In addition to developing traditional economic theories, Mill made substantial contributions by emphasising social justice and change. A large portion of classical economics was consolidated in his seminal work Principles of Political Economy (1848), which also addressed its flaws.

Key Theories of John Stuart Mill:

Utility and Utilitarianism: Mill was a proponent of utilitarianism, a philosophical theory that claims that the ideal behaviours are those that enhance total happiness or utility. This concept affected his economic reasoning, especially when it came to his support of social reforms that would enhance the welfare of the majority.

Role of Government: Even though Mill supported free markets, he acknowledged that there are situations when government involvement is necessary. He maintained that in addition to regulating monopolies and ensuring a more equitable distribution of income, the government should also provide public goods. Justice and fairness were important concerns to Mill, and he thought that the government should be involved in redressing the imbalances that result from an exclusively market-driven economy.

Theory of Production and Distribution: Mill distinguished the rules of production from the laws of distribution with great clarity. He maintained that whereas the laws of distribution are influenced by social and institutional variables, the laws of production are fixed and grounded in physical realities (such as the productivity of labour and capital). Because of this distinction, Mill was able to support changes in the wealth distribution without contesting the fundamentals of production.

Liberty and Individual Freedom: Apart from his financial contributions, Mill is renowned for his studies on individual liberty and freedom. He made the case that people should be allowed to follow their own interests as long as they do not damage others in his article On Liberty (1859). The emphasis on individual freedom aligns with the principles of classical economics, namely the value placed on voluntary transactions and self-interest.

To sum up, modern economic theory was developed with the help of classical economics. Its focus on free markets, recognition of the value of self-interest, and conviction that economies are self-regulating have influenced economic theory ever since. The field of economics was formed by the major contributions made by the classical economists, including Adam Smith, David Ricardo, Thomas Malthus, Jean-Baptiste Say, and John Stuart Mill.

The vast corpus of classical economic theory was enriched by the theories of Smith, Ricardo, Malthus, Say, Law of Markets, the invisible hand, division of labor, and individual liberty. In addition, Mill promoted social reform and individual liberty. Nevertheless, there were certain drawbacks to classical economics. With time, the emphasis on supply-side variables, the presumption of compell

Socialist

In its widest definition, socialist economics encompasses a variety of political and economic theories that support common or public ownership of the means of production and distribution of commodities and services. Socialist economists emphasise the necessity for equality, social welfare, and the elimination of class differences in their views, which frequently conflict with those of capitalist economics. Different socialist schools of thought have developed over time, with scholars presenting differing viewpoints on the means of achieving a more just economic structure. The contributions that notable socialist economists like Karl Marx, Friedrich Engels, Rosa Luxemburg, and Vladimir Lenin made to the socialist economic heritage will be discussed in this essay along with their theories.

Karl Marx (1818–1883)

Arguably, the most significant figure in socialist economic theory is Karl Marx. His writings served as the basis for the development of the theory known as Marxism, which opposes capitalist economies and calls for the destruction of capitalism in order to achieve a society without classes. Marx and Friedrich Engels co-wrote Das Kapital (1867) and The Communist Manifesto (1848), which both summarise his economic theories.

Key Theories of Karl Marx:

Historical Materialism: Marx's historical materialism thesis holds that society's social, political, and intellectual life is determined by its economic foundation, or mode of production. Marx argues that the tensions between the relations of production and the productive forces are what propel history as a sequence of class battles. This is seen in capitalist countries as a struggle between the proletariat (the working class) and the bourgeoisie (the capitalist class). Marx anticipated that this struggle would ultimately result in the demise of capitalism and the advent of socialism.

Labor Theory of Value: Marx embraced and expanded upon Adam Smith and David Ricardo's classical economic theories of labour and value. Marx argues that the quantity of socially essential labour time needed to produce a good or service determines its worth. But under capitalism, labourers receive a lower wage than the value they create, with capitalists keeping the excess value for themselves as profit. Marx maintained that class strife and capitalism's inherent instability stem from this exploitation.

Surplus Value and Exploitation: Marx's critique of capitalism revolves around the idea of surplus value. The difference between the value created by labour and the labourers' wages is known as surplus value. Workers create more value in capitalist production than they are paid for, and capitalists take this excess and turn it into profit. The working class becomes impoverished as a result of this exploitation process, which also results in the capitalist class gaining riches.

Commodity Fetishism: In order to describe how the value placed on commodities obscures social relationships in a capitalist society, Marx established the concept of commodity fetishism. The linkages between commodities in a capitalist economy obscure the interactions between people, such as those between labourers and capitalists. Marx maintained that workers grow separated from both each other and the products of their labour as a result of this fetishism.

Alienation: The alienation that workers in capitalist systems face was one of Marx's main concerns. He distinguished between four types of alienation: alienation from one's own species-being, or human nature; alienation from the act of production; alienation from other workers; and alienation from the end result of one's labour. Marx thought that this alienation would end under socialism, because the means of production would be owned jointly by the workers.

Marx argued that capitalism will ultimately collapse due to its inherent contradictions, which led to the Revolution and Dictatorship of the Proletariat. The working class would revolt, topple the capitalist order, and install a proletarian dictatorship as it grew more and more destitute and conscious of its exploitation. Class divisions and private property would be eliminated in this transitional state, ultimately paving the way for the creation of a communist society that was classless.

Friedrich Engels (1820–1895)

Friedrich Engels was a close collaborator of Karl Marx and played a significant role in developing and disseminating Marxist theory. He co-authored The Communist Manifesto and contributed to many of Marx's later works. Engels also wrote several important works on his own, including The Condition of the Working Class in England (1845) and Anti-Dühring (1878).

Key Theories of Friedrich Engels:

Class Struggle and Social Revolution: Like Marx, Engels believed that history is defined by class struggle. He argued that the working class must rise up against the capitalist class to establish socialism. Engels emphasised that socialism could not be achieved through gradual reforms but required a revolutionary transformation of society.

Dialectics of Nature: Engels expanded upon Marxist theory by applying dialectical materialism to the natural sciences. In Dialectics of Nature, he argued that nature, like society, operates according to dialectical laws—thesis, antithesis, and synthesis—which drive change and development. This work aimed to demonstrate the scientific basis of Marxist theory and to counter bourgeois idealism.

Role of the State: Engels, in works such as The Origin of the Family, Private Property, and the State, argued that the state emerged historically to serve the interests of the ruling class. In a capitalist society, the state is an instrument of the bourgeoisie used to maintain its dominance over the proletariat. Like Marx, Engels believed that after the proletariat seized power, the state would eventually wither away as class distinctions were abolished.

Rosa Luxemburg (1871–1919)

Rosa Luxemburg was a prominent Marxist theorist and revolutionary socialist who criticised both capitalist and reformist socialist movements. She was a leader of the German Social Democratic Party (SPD) and later co-founded the Spartacus League, which became the Communist Party of Germany (KPD). Luxemburg is best known for her works The Accumulation of Capital (1913) and Reform or Revolution (1899).

Key Theories of Rosa Luxemburg:

Critique of Reformism: In Reform or Revolution, Luxemburg criticised the reformist tendencies within the socialist movement, particularly those advocated by Eduard Bernstein. Bernstein and his followers believed that socialism could be achieved gradually through parliamentary reforms within the capitalist system. Luxemburg argued that this approach was flawed because capitalism could not be reformed; it had to be overthrown through revolutionary means. She emphasised that only the working class, through mass action and revolution, could bring about socialism.

The Accumulation of Capital: In her major theoretical work, The Accumulation of Capital, Luxemburg sought to explain the causes of imperialism and capitalist crises. She argued that capitalism requires non-capitalist markets to survive, as it needs external markets to absorb surplus goods and capital. However, as capitalism expands globally, these non-capitalist markets are absorbed, leading to economic crises and the eventual collapse of the capitalist system. This analysis was a significant contribution to Marxist theory and helped explain the economic motivations behind imperialism.

Mass Strike and Revolution: Luxemburg was a strong advocate of the mass strike as a means of revolutionary struggle. She believed that spontaneous mass strikes, driven by the working class, could lead to revolutionary upheaval. Her writings on the mass strike influenced revolutionary movements in Europe and distinguished her from other Marxists who emphasised more centralised forms of political action.

Vladimir Lenin (1870–1924)

Vladimir Lenin was a Russian revolutionary leader and the key figure in the development of Marxism-Leninism, the dominant form of socialist theory in the 20th century. His writings and leadership in the Russian Revolution of 1917 laid the foundation for the establishment of the Soviet Union. Lenin's major works include What Is to Be Done? (1902), The State and Revolution (1917), and Imperialism, the Highest Stage of Capitalism (1916).

Key Theories of Vladimir Lenin:

Theory of Imperialism: In Imperialism, the Highest Stage of Capitalism, Lenin argued that imperialism was a necessary and final stage of capitalist development. He expanded on Marx's theory of capitalism by showing that capitalist economies, in search of new markets and resources, inevitably lead to imperialist expansion. According to Lenin, the competition among capitalist nations for control of foreign markets and colonies would lead to conflicts and wars, ultimately hastening the collapse of capitalism.

Democratic Centralism: Lenin developed the concept of democratic centralism as a form of organizational structure for revolutionary socialist parties. Democratic centralism emphasised centralized leadership and discipline within the party, with decisions made by a small group of leaders after internal debate. This was necessary, according to Lenin, to ensure the effectiveness of the revolutionary movement and to avoid the fragmentation of the working class.

Dictatorship of the Proletariat: Lenin expanded on Marx's idea of the dictatorship of the proletariat, arguing that the working class, after seizing power, would need to establish a dictatorship to suppress the bourgeoisie and defend the revolution. This dictatorship would be a transitional phase on the path to socialism, during which the state would control the economy and the means of production.

New Classicals

Neoclassical economics is one of the most dominant schools of thought in current economics, that specialize in how people make selections in situations of scarcity and the way those decisions interact inside markets to allocate resources correctly. Rising in the late 19th century, neoclassical economics built on the foundations of classical economics, specifically those laid out by Adam Smith and David Ricardo, but brought key adjustments. It focuses heavily on individual decision-making, the function of utility and rationality, and market equilibrium. Prominent figures in this culture include William Stanley Jevons, Carl Menger, Léon Walras, Alfred Marshall, and later economists including John Hicks and Paul Samuelson.

This essay will explore the theories of these prominent neoclassical economists, inspecting their contributions and the overall framework of neoclassical economics.

William Stanley Jevons (1835–1882)

William Stanley Jevons became one of the founders of the neoclassical faculty and is satisfactorily regarded for developing the theory of marginal software, which has become a cornerstone of neoclassical economics. His major painting, The Theory of Political Economy (1871), laid the muse for a lot of present-day economic notions by way of focusing on how individuals make intake picks based totally on marginal utility.

Key Theories of William Stanley Jevons:

Marginal application: Jevons argued that the fee of a great is determined not with the aid of the entire utility it affords but by using the application of the final unit ate up—what he known as marginal utility. As individuals consume extra of an excellent, the utility derived from each additional unit declines, mainly due to the regulation of diminishing marginal utility. This perception changed into revolutionary as it shifted monetary ideas from focusing on the cost of manufacturing (as in classical economics) to the subjective price located on items with the aid of customers.

Concept of exchange: Jevons also advanced a theory of exchange based on marginal utility. He argued that individuals interact in exchange because they value goods in another way. By way of buying and selling, they could each improve their well-being. In a free market, the change ratio (or rate) of goods will be regulated until the marginal application of the goods is equalized for both events. This concept laid the foundation for cutting-edge theories of delivery and called for.

Mathematical method: Jevons changed into a pioneer in applying mathematical strategies to economics. He believed that economic behaviour might be modelled using mathematical equations, which might permit extra unique predictions and deeper expertise in economic phenomena. His paintings contributed to the growing formalization of economics, a fashion that would maintain at some point in the twentieth century.

Carl Menger (1840–1921)

Carl Menger, the founding father of the Austrian College of Economics, is another key discern in the improvement of neoclassical economics. His fundamental work, *Principles of Economics* (1871), introduced the idea of marginal utility independently of Jevons and laid the groundwork for Austrian economics, which emphasizes the importance of man or woman selections and the subjective nature of price.

Key Theories of Carl Menger:

The subjective idea of fee: Menger argued that fees aren't inherent in items; however, they are alternatives decided by the importance individuals have on them. This subjective theory of fee was a departure from the labour theory of value championed by classical economists like

Adam Smith and David Ricardo. In keeping with Menger, the cost of an awesome depends on its ability to fulfil human desires, and this cost can vary from individual to character.

Marginal application and rate Formation: Like Jevons, Menger emphasized the role of marginal application in determining fees. He argued that individuals make economic decisions based on the additional pleasure (or utility) they receive from eating one more unit of a very good. This idea is significant to information on how expenses are shaped in markets, as the rate of a very good will adjust till it reflects the marginal software consumers derive from it.

The idea of cash: Menger also made essential contributions to the theory of cash. He argued that money emerges spontaneously in a marketplace economic system as people are seeking to change items more successfully. In step with Menger, cash is not an introduction of the nation, but instead, a made of the herbal evolution of alternate. Through the years, positive items (such as gold or silver) have grown to be widely popular as mediums of exchange due to their desirability, divisibility, and durability.

Léon Walras (1834–1910)

Léon Walras, a French economist, is first-rate regarded for growing the theory of standard equilibrium, which seeks to explain how all markets in an economy engage to attain a kingdom of stability. His most influential painting, elements of Pure Economics (1874), was a milestone within the formalization of economics and laid the muse for an awful lot of modern microeconomics.

Key Theories of Léon Walras:

Standard Equilibrium principle: Walras' trendy equilibrium idea is one of the cornerstones of neoclassical economics. He sought to illustrate that, in a competitive marketplace, all markets (for items, services, labour, and Capital) will attain equilibrium concurrently. Walras used a machine of equations to model how prices and portions adjust in exceptional markets till delivery equals demand in all. This concept of interrelated markets became groundbreaking and laid the inspiration for a great deal of modern-day financial ideas, inclusive of later developments in macroeconomics.

Tâtonnement process: Walras introduced the concept of the tâtonnement (French for "groping") process to explain how markets obtain equilibrium. In this method, a fictional auctioneer adjusts charges based totally on extra supply or calls for in distinctive markets. While there may be an excess demand for a good, the price rises, and whilst there may be an extra delivery, the fee falls. This keeps till the market clears, which means that delivery equals a call for in all markets. Whilst the tâtonnement process is a theoretical construct, it offers a framework for information on how markets circulate closer to equilibrium.

Mathematical Economics: Walras became a robust advocate for the use of arithmetic in economics. He believed that economics may be dealt with as a technological know-how, with laws and equations governing financial conduct. His paintings paved the way for the later formalization of financial fashions and using calculus and linear algebra in monetary analysis.

Alfred Marshall (1842–1924)

Alfred Marshall is considered one of the most influential economists of the overdue nineteenth and early twentieth centuries. His textbook concepts of Economics (1890) have become the standard reference for economists for many, many years and synthesized the various key insights of neoclassical economics. Marshall is, in particular, recognized for his improvement of delivery and demand analysis, elasticity, and the concept of client surplus.

Key Theories of Alfred Marshall:

Supply and demand: Marshall is most well-known for his graphical illustration of supply and call for curves, which illustrate how charges are determined in a competitive market. The intersection of the supply and call-for curves represents the marketplace equilibrium, wherein the quantity demanded by purchasers equals the quantity furnished by means of producers. Marshall's version remains one of the most widely used equipment in economics and is significant to the microeconomic ideas.

Elasticity: Marshall introduced the concept of elasticity to the degree of responsiveness of customers and producers to adjustments in rate. Fee elasticity of call for measures the share exchange in the amount demanded of a terrific in response to a per cent change in its fee. Items with high elasticity (which include luxurious items) enjoy significant changes in demand whilst costs differ, whilst goods with low elasticity (inclusive of necessities) revel in smaller modifications in call for. Elasticity is an essential idea for expertise in consumer behaviour and marketplace dynamics.

Patron Surplus: Marshall also advanced the concept of client surplus, which measures the difference between what consumers are willing to pay for a very good and what they, in reality, pay. Customer surplus is in the vicinity below the call-for-the-curve; however, it is above the marketplace price. It represents the extra advantage clients acquire from shopping for goods at decreased charges than they would be inclined to pay. This concept is crucial for welfare economics, as it provides a way to measure the benefits that purchasers derive from market transactions.

Partial Equilibrium Analysis: even as Walras centred on popular equilibrium, Marshall advanced the idea of partial equilibrium analysis, which examines the equilibrium of an unmarried marketplace in isolation from the relaxation of the economic system. Marshall believed that this approach changed into extra sensible for studying real-global markets, as it allowed economists to be cognizant of the interactions among supply and call for in specific industries while not having to don't forget the whole economy.

John Hicks (1904–1989)

John Hicks turned into one of the maximum influential economists of the 20th century, known for his contributions to both microeconomics and macroeconomics. His work, value and Capital (1939), helped formalize the concept of well-known equilibrium and introduced crucial thoughts consisting of the IS-LM model, which have become critical to Keynesian economics.

Key Theories of John Hicks:

IS-LM version: Hicks is nicely acknowledged for developing the IS-LM version, which became a relevant framework for Keynesian economics. The IS-LM model (investment-saving, Liquidity preference-money delivery) represents the interaction between the products marketplace (IS curve) and the cash marketplace (LM curve). It suggests how changes in economic coverage (government spending and taxes) and economic coverage (hobby quotes and cash delivery) can have an effect on the equilibrium degree of income and interest costs. At the same time, this version was designed to give an explanation for short-time period fluctuations inside the financial system, and it additionally furnished a bridge between neoclassical and Keynesian economics.

Hicksian call for: Hicks additionally made large contributions to the purchaser's ideas. He advanced the concept of Hicksian call for, which distinguishes between the earnings and substitution effects of a fee trade. When the fee changes, customers alter their consumption because of both a trade in their real income (profits impact) and an exchange in the relative fee of goods (substitution effect). Hicksian call for curves to hold actual income regular and isolate

New Classicals

New Classical Economics is a modern school of thought in macroeconomics that emerged in the 1970s as a response to Keynesian economics, advocating a return to the principles of classical economics, but with more sophisticated tools like rational expectations and general equilibrium models. New classical economists emphasize the importance of microeconomic foundations for understanding macroeconomic phenomena. Unlike Keynesian economists, who believe in active government intervention to smooth business cycles, new classical economists argue that markets are generally self-regulating, and government interference often causes more harm than good.

Key figures associated with new classical economics include Robert Lucas, Edward Prescott, Finn Kydland, Thomas Sargent, and John Muth. Their work on rational expectations, real business cycle theory, and the inefficacy of monetary policy in the long run has shaped modern macroeconomic theory. This essay will explore their key contributions to new classical economics, highlighting their critiques of Keynesianism and their impact on economic policy and thought.

John Muth (1930–2005)

John Muth is considered the originator of the rational expectations hypothesis, which has become a cornerstone of new classical economics. His seminal paper, Rational Expectations and the Theory of Price Movements (1961), laid the groundwork for a new way of thinking about expectations in economic models.

Key Theories of John Muth:

Rational Expectations: Muth argued that economic agents (individuals and firms) form expectations about the future in a rational way, using all available information. This contrasts with adaptive expectations, which assume that people base their expectations solely on past experiences. According to Muth, individuals and firms use all relevant information, including knowledge of economic policies, to make predictions about future events. Thus, they do not systematically make mistakes when forecasting variables like inflation or interest rates.

Rational expectations have significant implications for economic policy. If people anticipate the effects of monetary or fiscal policy, they will adjust their behaviour accordingly, potentially neutralising the impact of the policy. For instance, if the government tries to reduce unemployment by increasing the money supply, workers might anticipate higher inflation and demand higher wages, negating the stimulative effect on employment.

Muth's work on rational expectations laid the foundation for later developments in macroeconomic theory, particularly in the hands of Robert Lucas and other new classical economists.

Robert Lucas (1937–2023)

Robert Lucas is arguably the most influential figure in the development of new classical economics. His work on rational expectations and the Lucas critique fundamentally changed the way economists think about macroeconomic policy. Lucas was awarded the Nobel Prize in Economics in 1995 for his contributions to the development and application of the rational expectations hypothesis and his work on the theory of business cycles.

Key Theories of Robert Lucas:

Lucas Critique: In his famous paper Econometric Policy Evaluation: A Critique (1976), Lucas argued that traditional macroeconomic models, such as those used by Keynesians, were flawed because they did not account for changes in expectations when policies change. According to

Lucas, any attempt to use historical data to predict the effects of a policy change would be unreliable, as individuals and firms would adjust their expectations in response to the policy itself.

For example, if a central bank follows a policy of reducing inflation by raising interest rates, individuals and firms will not simply react to the new interest rates based on past behaviour. Instead, they will form new expectations based on the central bank's commitment to lower inflation in the future. This means that policy analysis must take into account how people's expectations change in response to the policy, a key insight that reshaped macroeconomic modelling.

Rational Expectations and Market Efficiency: Building on Muth's work, Lucas applied the rational expectations hypothesis to a range of macroeconomic issues. He argued that markets are generally efficient, meaning that prices reflect all available information. As a result, attempts by policymakers to influence economic outcomes, such as inflation or output, would be largely ineffective unless they were unexpected. Once people anticipate the effects of a policy, they adjust their behaviour, and the policy loses its impact.

This insight led Lucas to question the effectiveness of Keynesian demand management policies. According to Lucas, the only way for monetary or fiscal policy to have a real effect on the economy is if it takes people by surprise. However, because individuals are rational and forward-looking, such surprises are rare.

Lucas Supply Curve: Lucas also developed a supply-side theory to explain short-run fluctuations in output and employment. He argued that workers and firms cannot always distinguish between changes in the overall price level and changes in relative prices. As a result, when the price level rises unexpectedly, workers may believe that the relative price of their labour has increased, leading them to supply more labour. This temporary misperception leads to short-run increases in output and employment. However, once people realise that the price increase was general (i.e., inflation), they adjust their expectations, and the economy returns to its natural level of output and employment.

This idea was encapsulated in the "Lucas supply curve," which explains short-term deviations from full employment in response to unexpected changes in the price level. However, in the long run, when expectations adjust, the economy returns to full employment, meaning that there is no long-term trade-off between inflation and unemployment.

Edward Prescott (1940–2022) and Finn Kydland (1943)

Edward Prescott and Finn Kydland are best known for their development of real business cycle (RBC) theory, which argues that economic fluctuations are largely the result of real shocks, such as changes in technology, rather than changes in demand or monetary policy. They were jointly awarded the Nobel Prize in Economics in 2004 for their contributions to dynamic macroeconomics, particularly the time inconsistency of economic policy and the driving forces behind business cycles.

Key Theories of Edward Prescott and Finn Kydland:

Real Business Cycle Theory: Traditional Keynesian models attribute economic fluctuations to changes in aggregate demand, often driven by monetary or fiscal policy. In contrast, Prescott and Kydland argued that business cycles are primarily caused by real shocks, such as changes in technology or productivity. Their work, particularly their paper *Time to Build and Aggregate Fluctuations* (1982), provided a model in which economic fluctuations are the natural result of changes in the productivity of capital and labor.

According to RBC theory, when a positive productivity shock occurs (such as a technological innovation), firms become more productive, leading to higher output and wages. Conversely, when a negative shock occurs (such as a rise in oil prices), productivity falls, leading to lower output and employment. These fluctuations are not the result of demand-side factors, like changes in government spending or interest rates, but rather reflect the efficient response of the economy to changes in the real environment.

Time Consistency and Economic Policy: In their influential paper Rules Rather Than Discretion: The Inconsistency of Optimal Plans (1977), Kydland and Prescott demonstrated that policymakers face a "time consistency problem." They argued that economic policy is more effective when it follows consistent, predictable rules rather than being subject to discretionary changes. This is because individuals and firms form expectations based on the assumption that policymakers will stick to their announced policies.

For example, if a central bank commits to keeping inflation low, individuals will form expectations of low inflation and adjust their behavior accordingly (e.g., setting long-term contracts with low wage increases). However, if the central bank later abandons this commitment and allows inflation to rise, individuals will lose trust in future commitments, leading to higher inflation expectations and more volatility in the economy.

This insight had significant implications for monetary policy. It suggested that central banks should commit to rules (such as inflation targeting) to avoid the time consistency problem and enhance the credibility of their policies.

Thomas Sargent (1943)

Thomas Sargent is one of the leading figures in the development of new classical economics, particularly in the areas of rational expectations, monetary policy, and the theory of economic policy. Sargent's work, including his contributions to the understanding of policy ineffectiveness, helped reshape modern macroeconomics.

Key Theories of Thomas Sargent:

Policy Ineffectiveness Proposition: Sargent, along with Neil Wallace, developed the policy ineffectiveness proposition, which argues that systematic monetary policy cannot influence real economic variables like output or employment in the long run. This is because individuals form rational expectations about future policy actions, meaning that any predictable policy will already be factored into their behaviour.

For example, if the central bank consistently increases the money supply to reduce unemployment, workers and firms will anticipate higher inflation and adjust their wage demands and prices accordingly. As a result, the increase in the money supply will lead to higher inflation without reducing unemployment. This insight challenged the Keynesian view that monetary policy could be used to manage the economy in the long run.

Rational Expectations and Inflation: Sargent's work on inflation and hyperinflation demonstrated how expectations play a critical role in the dynamics of inflation. In his book The Ends of Four Big Inflations (1983), Sargent analysed historical episodes of hyperinflation in countries like Germany and Hungary and showed that inflation can only be controlled when governments commit to credible monetary policies. When people expect inflation to continue, they act in ways that perpetuate it (e.g., by demanding higher wages or raising prices). However, once governments commit to stable policies, inflation expectations adjust, and inflation can be brought under control.

Dynamic Stochastic General Equilibrium (DSGE) Models: Sargent also played a key role in the development of dynamic stochastic general equilibrium (DSGE) models, which have become the standard tool for analysing macroeconomic fluctuations. These models incorporate rational expectations, real shocks, and market-clearing behaviour to explain how economies respond to changes in technology, policy, and other factors. DSGE models provide a microeconomic foundation for macro.

Other Economic Theories

The Kalecki Principle

The Kalecki Principle, developed by means of economist Michal Kalecki, offers a completely unique perspective on the dynamics of profits, funding, and demand in an economy. Unlike classical economics, which often emphasizes supply-side factors, Kalecki's method highlights the important role of demand and expectations in driving monetary interest. This essay explores the central tenets of the Kalecki principle, its implications for understanding monetary fluctuations, and its relevance to modern monetary discourse.

Historical background on Michal Kalecki.

Michal Kalecki (1899–1970) was a Polish economist whose work predates and parallels John Maynard Keynes. While Keynes focused on aggregate demand and its consequences on employment and output, Kalecki emphasized the role of investment and its relation to income and economic cycles. His theories are often seen as a bridge between classical and modern macroeconomic thought, incorporating elements of both.

Key concepts of the Kalecki principle

Earnings and investment: Kalecki argued that earnings in an economic system are in general decided via the level of investment. While corporations invest, they invent new ability, which in turn generates income for workers and suppliers. This income results in improved intake, further boosting demand and doubtlessly ensuing in greater earnings.

Effective demand: Critical to Kalecki's theory is the concept of effective demand. He posited that overall demand in a financial system is driven by means of the choices of companies to invest. In a capitalist economic system, investment is influenced by the expectations of future demand. If businesses assume demand to rise, they may be much more likely to invest, thereby increasing income.

Function of commercial enterprise expectancies: Kalecki highlighted the significance of business expectations in shaping funding choices. Firms regularly depend on past reviews and current monetary conditions to forecast future demand. If corporations count on a downturn, they will cut back on investment, leading to a self-fulfilling prophecy of decreased monetary interest.

The anomaly of Thrift: Kalecki's precept also ties into the ambiguity of thrift, in which elevated saving by way of individuals at some stage in monetary uncertainty can lead to a decrease in standard call for. While families store more, consumption declines, prompting agencies to reduce funding, ultimately resulting in lower profits and potentially higher unemployment.

Distribution of earnings: Every other vital aspect of the Kalecki precept is its attention on income distribution. Kalecki argued that the distribution of profits among wages and income affects consumption patterns. Higher income generally tends to accrue to capital proprietors, who are much less likely to spend than workers. Hence, earnings inequality can prevent average demand in the economy.

Implications of the Kalecki Precept

Understanding Financial Cycles: The Kalecki precept provides a framework for expertise monetary cycles. During durations of increase, growing earnings encourage investment, which fuels further calls for economic enlargement. Conversely, at some point in a recession, falling income causes reduced investment and declining demand, creating a downward spiral.

Policy tips: Kalecki's insights recommend that government intervention is necessary to stabilize financial fluctuations. By way of stimulating calls for monetary guidelines, together with expanded government spending or tax cuts, governments can counteract the poor consequences of reduced investment during downturns.

Investment as a coverage tool: Kalecki's principle posits that funding selections are encouraged by government regulations. Regulations that promote enterprise confidence, consisting of infrastructure investment or tax incentives, can enhance expectancies of future calls, leading to elevated investment and economic boom.

Critique of Classical monetary models: The Kalecki precept demands classical financial fashions that prioritize deliver-aspect elements. It emphasizes that profits and funding are not solely decided by using market mechanisms but are substantially encouraged with the aid of calls for dynamics and enterprise expectancies.

Relevance to modern issues: The Kalecki precept remains applicable in discussions of contemporary financial challenges, together with profit inequality, unemployment, and the role of monetary coverage. As economies grapple with the aftereffects of financial crises, Kalecki's recognition of demand-driven growth gives precious insights.

Evaluations and obstacles: Even as the Kalecki principle presents a compelling framework for information economic conduct, it isn't always without reviews. Some economists argue that it oversimplifies the complexities of investment decisions and does now not properly account for the role of outside factors, including international monetary situations and technological improvements.

Moreover, the emphasis on the call may additionally neglect the supply-aspect constraints that can also impact the monetary boom. Critics contend that a balanced technique, incorporating both demand and supply elements, is vital for a comprehensive knowledge of monetary dynamics.

To sum up, The Kalecki principle gives an important angle on the relationship between income, funding, and effective demand. Via emphasizing the function of commercial enterprise expectancies and income distribution, Kalecki's principle demands situations of conventional monetary models and gives insights that continue to be applicable in today's economic discourse. Information on the dynamics of demand-driven increase is essential for policymakers aiming to navigate financial fluctuations and foster sustainable improvement. As the global economic system continues to adapt, revisiting Kalecki's standards can remove darkness from pathways for addressing cutting-edge economic challenges.

The Paradox of Thrift

The paradox of thrift is a giant concept in macroeconomics, illustrating the complicated relationship between man or woman saving conduct and normal economic health. Coined by John Maynard Keynes, this paradox highlights the counterintuitive nature of saving at some point of monetary downturns. While saving is generally seen as a prudent financial decision for individuals, when adopted throughout a recession, it is able to cause unfavorable financial results, along with decreased aggregate demand, lower manufacturing, and extended unemployment. This essay delves into the mechanics of the ambiguity of thrift, its implications for economic policy, and its relevance in cutting-edge monetary discourse.

Understanding the ambiguity

At its core, the anomaly of thrift shows that while increased saving can benefit people and families, it is able to simultaneously harm the economic system when all people attempt to store extra without delay. Throughout economic uncertainty, individuals may additionally choose to keep more as a precaution against future financial instability. This conduct appears rational; but, when a large number of humans undertake this attitude, the collective result can lead to reduced spending and decrease average demand for goods and services.

Mechanisms of the paradox

Decreased intake: When customers decide to keep more, their immediate spending decreases. Since consumer spending accounts for a significant part of aggregate demand, this reduction can result in a decline in business revenues. As a result, companies may respond by reducing back on production, leading to layoffs or reduced hours for employees.

Lower business investment: As businesses see a drop in consumer demand, their confidence in future income diminishes. Therefore, companies may reduce or delay investments in capital, such as new equipment or expansion. This decrease in investment further exacerbates the economic downturn, creating a vicious cycle.

Growing Unemployment: As companies reduce production and investment, they often lay off employees or freeze hiring. Increased unemployment results in even lower consumer spending, as fewer people have disposable income. This cycle of rising unemployment and decreasing demand can deepen the recession.

Effect on monetary increase: The anomaly highlights a broader problem: a prolonged cognizance on saving can stifle economic boom. In a healthful financial system, a stability between saving and spending is important. Immoderate saving during downturns can preclude recovery efforts and slow the return to monetary stability.

Historic Context: The ambiguity of thrift won prominence all through the awesome depression of the Nineteen Thirties. In the wake of extensive financial problem, many individuals and households opted to keep greater, fearing in addition financial fall apart. This collective conduct contributed to prolonged economic stagnation, as reduced intake deepened the crisis. Keynes emphasized that authority's intervention was crucial to stimulate demand and counteract the outcomes of the paradox.

Coverage Implications: Know-how the anomaly of thrift has large implications for economic policy, especially all through recessions. Policymakers can take several procedures to mitigate the terrible outcomes of increased saving.

Monetary Stimulus: Governments can implement economic policies, along with elevated public spending or direct monetary help to households, to stimulate demand. By injecting money into the economy, governments can encourage consumption even if individual saving rates are high.

Financial policy: Vital banks can lower hobby fees to make borrowing cheaper, encouraging both purchaser spending and commercial enterprise investment. Lower quotes can incentivize individuals to spend in preference to save, hence counteracting the decline in combination calls.

Public Recognition Campaigns: Teaching the general public about the financial impacts of the anomaly of thrift can assist in tempering immoderate saving behaviours at some stage in downturns. By highlighting the importance of preserving stability among saving and spending, policymakers can foster more stable monetary surroundings.

Assist for prone Populations: During financial downturns, centred help for the one's maximum affected—along with the unemployed or low-earnings families—can help maintain intake ranges. Applications that offer food help, unemployment benefits, and housing support can alleviate the pressure on these families and inspire endured spending.

Relevance today

The anomaly of thrift remains applicable in cutting-edge monetary discussions, especially inside the context of the latest international monetary challenges, along with the COVID-19 pandemic. In the course of the pandemic, many people accelerated their financial savings in reaction to uncertainty and economic shutdowns. Governments internationally answered with unparalleled fiscal measures to aid economies and inspire intake.

For instance, stimulus assessments and more desirable unemployment benefits have been carried out in many nations to save you a pointy decline in spending. Those measures aimed to counteract the paradox of thrift by at once injecting cash into the financial system, thereby selling customer spending even if people have been willing to store it.

Evaluations and boundaries: At the same time, as the paradox of thrift affords treasured insights into the interplay between saving and financial hobby, it's critical to understand its boundaries. Critics argue that the idea may additionally oversimplify the complexities of economic behaviour. Not all savings are adverse; for instance, expanded savings can provide a buffer for destiny monetary shocks or fund productive investments.

Additionally, the anomaly assumes a closed financial system where home spending is the number one driver of demand. In a globalized economy, external factors such as trade balances, overseas investments, and global demand can also have an effect on average monetary conditions.

To sum up, the anomaly of thrift illustrates the problematic courting between a person's economic behaviour and broader monetary consequences. At the same time, saving is generally regarded as a wonderful motion; collective saving at some stage in monetary downturns can result in decreased calls for lower manufacturing and better unemployment. Know-how this paradox is vital for effective monetary coverage, mainly in times of crisis. By implementing measures that stimulate calls for and inspire spending, policymakers can mitigate the unfavourable outcomes of the paradox of thrift and promote a greater stable monetary healing. As the global economy maintains uncertainties, revisiting the training of ambiguity stays essential for fostering resilience and sustainable growth.

Chaos Theory in Economics

Chaos theory, traditionally related to the herbal sciences, has located good-sized software in the discipline of economics, providing treasured insights into the complicated and regularly unpredictable conduct of monetary systems. This essay delves into the fundamental standards of chaos theory, its relevance to financial phenomena, and its implications for financial modeling and policy-making.

Chaos theory studies systems that are distinctly sensitive to preliminary conditions, frequently defined as the "butterfly effect," in which small adjustments can cause hugely exclusive results. Unlike linear systems, wherein cause and impact are predictable, chaotic structures exhibit nonlinear dynamics, making long-term predictions tremendously tough.

In economics, chaos theory challenges the notion of equilibrium and the predictability of economic conduct, suggesting that economies may additionally function underneath chaotic conditions due to the interaction of several variables and agents.

Key ideas in Chaos theory

Sensitivity to preliminary situations: In chaotic structures, slight variations in initial conditions can lead to divergent consequences. In monetary phrases, this means that small shocks—such as changes in consumer confidence or unexpected policy announcements—could have profound consequences on the economy.

Nonlinearity: Financial relationships are often nonlinear, meaning that the impact of a variable on an outcome is not steady. For instance, the effect of interest rate changes on investment may vary depending on the current economic environment. This nonlinearity complicates the method of correct financial models.

Attractors: Chaos theory introduces the concept of attractors, which might be states toward which a system tends to adapt. In economics, attractors may also represent strong points or cycles within a financial system, even in the presence of chaotic behavior.

Fractals: Fractals are complex systems that exhibit self-similarity across different scales. In economics, fractal patterns may be found in financial markets, where price movements show similar patterns over diverse time frames, indicating underlying chaotic processes.

Applications of Chaos theory in Economics

Economic Markets: Chaos theory has been notably applied to analyse financial markets, which often display unstable and unpredictable behaviour. Research has shown that stock prices and market indices can showcase chaotic dynamics, complicating the task of forecasting marketplace movements. Understanding these dynamics enables investors to develop strategies to navigate market fluctuations.

Business Cycles: The behaviour of business cycles can also be interpreted through the lens of chaos theory. Traditional models often assume smooth oscillations around an equilibrium. However, chaos theory indicates that business cycles may be irregular and unpredictable, influenced by various internal and external factors.

Monetary growth: Chaos principle has been used to examine the dynamics of monetary boom. Models incorporating chaotic conduct can better provide an explanation for surprising shifts in growth trajectories and the emergence of latest boom styles, though the conventional know-how of solid growth paths.

Agent-based totally Modeling: Agent-based modeling (ABMs) simulate the interactions of man or woman marketers within an economic system, allowing for the emergence of complex behaviors. These models often display chaotic dynamics that are not apparent in conventional aggregate models, providing insights into how micro-level interactions can impact macroeconomic results.

Challenges and boundaries

Complexity of models: Developing correct chaotic fashions calls for state-of-the-art mathematical tools and a deep know-how of the underlying monetary techniques. This complexity can limit the practical application of chaos idea in policy-making.

Statistics barriers: The empirical validation of chaotic models frequently faces challenges because of restrained records availability and the problem of as it should be shooting economic dynamics. Ancient statistics might not fully constitute the complexities of cutting-edge monetary situations.

Interpretation of consequences: The consequences obtained from chaos-based models can be hard to interpret. Policymakers may also struggle to derive actionable insights from findings that highlight the unpredictability of monetary structures.

Implications for economic policy

Understanding the consequences of chaos theory in economics can substantially impact policy-making:

Adaptive regulations: Policymakers need to adopt adaptive strategies that are flexible and aware of changing financial situations. Recognising the potential for chaotic conduct encourages a dynamic approach to policy components, rather than rigid adherence to predetermined plans.

Consciousness on Resilience: Emphasising resilience rather than balance is vital in chaotic structures. Regulations must aim to enhance the economic system's potential to withstand shocks and recover from disruptions, promoting long-term sustainability.

Monitoring indicators: Policymakers should monitor a broader range of monetary indicators to capture the complexities of chaotic behaviour. Understanding the interaction of various factors can help identify emerging trends and inform timely interventions.

Collaboration across Disciplines: The interdisciplinary nature of chaos theory requires collaboration among economists, mathematicians, and systems theorists. Engaging diverse perspectives can result in more robust models and insights into economic dynamics.

To sum up, the Chaos theory provides a treasured framework for know-how of the complex and often unpredictable conduct of economic systems. By emphasizing the sensitivity to preliminary conditions, nonlinearity, and the emergence of chaotic dynamics, this idea challenges conventional monetary paradigms that depend upon equilibrium assumptions. As economies keep evolving in an increasing number of interconnected and complex international, embracing the insights of chaos principle can enhance our expertise in financial behaviour and inform powerful coverage-making. The popularity that economies might also function under chaotic conditions underscores the significance of flexibility, resilience, and flexibility in economic techniques.

Institutional Economics

Institutional economics is a branch of economics that emphasizes the role of establishments—defined as the formal and informal rules, norms, and structures that form human behaviour—in influencing financial outcomes. This technique diverges from conventional economic theories that focus attention more often than not on individual alternatives and market mechanisms. By analyzing how institutions affect overall financial performance, institutional economics gives treasured insights into the complexities of economic structures and the strategies of trade.

Ancient Context

The roots of institutional economics can be traced back to the early 20th century, with influential figures such as Thorstein Veblen, John R. Commons, and Wesley Mitchell. Veblen criticized the neoclassical monetary awareness of character rationality and software maximization, emphasizing alternatively the significance of social and cultural elements in shaping monetary conduct. Commons delivered the concept of collective action and the significance of institutions in coordinating monetary activities. Wesley Mitchell contributed to the empirical evaluation of financial phenomena, advocating for a more comprehensive expertise of monetary dynamics.

Within the late 20th century, the paintings of economists, including Douglass North and Oliver Williamson, further advanced institutional economics. North's emphasis on the function of institutions in economic development and Williamson's recognition of transaction prices furnished a theoretical framework for analyzing how institutions have an effect on monetary behaviour.

Ideas of Institutional Economics

Institutions as Constraints and Facilitators: Establishments serve both as constraints on behaviour and as facilitators of monetary pastimes.

They offer the policies of the sport that form interactions among financial sellers, influencing their selections and strategies. Institutions can include felony frameworks, asset rights, social norms, and cultural practices.

Transaction expenses: A relevant concept in institutional economics is transaction costs, which are the fees related to carrying out monetary exchanges. These expenses can consist of seek and data fees, bargaining and choice charges, and enforcement prices. Institutional preparations are regularly designed to minimize transaction prices, thereby facilitating economic cooperation and trade.

Route Dependence: Institutional economics emphasizes the idea of path dependence, which indicates that historical events and decisions will have long-lasting outcomes on current financial outcomes. As soon as a specific institutional framework is hooked up, it may end up self-reinforcing, making it tough to change or transition to alternative arrangements.

Co-evolution of institutions and financial behaviour: Institutions and economic conduct are visible as co-evolving, which means that modifications in you'll be able to result in changes inside the different. As economic practices and technology evolve, establishments must additionally adapt to deal with those adjustments. This dynamic interaction shapes the trajectory of financial improvement.

Position of records: Institutional economics places a sturdy emphasis on ancient context. Monetary consequences cannot be completely understood without thinking about the ancient evolution of institutions and the socio-political environments in which they function.

Applications of Institutional Economics

Monetary improvement: Institutional economics offers insights into the elements that pressure financial development. International locations with robust, properly-defined institutions that promote property rights, reduce transaction costs and inspire investment generally tend to experience better stages of financial increase. Conversely, susceptible establishments can avoid development and contribute to poverty.

Comparative Institutional analysis: This method lets in for the comparison of various institutional frameworks throughout countries and regions. through reading how various institutions have an effect on economic performance, researchers can pick out exceptional practices and capacity reforms to improve financial consequences.

Company Governance: Institutional economics has implications for company governance, becausethe systems and practices within corporations are inspired via the broader institutional surroundings. knowledge how specific governance mechanisms interact with institutional factors can help enhance company performance and responsibility.

Environmental Economics: The position of establishments in dealing with commonplace resources and addressing environmental issues is a key place of hobby in institutional economics. Powerful establishments can facilitate cooperation amongst stakeholders, sell sustainable practices, and beautify useful resource management.

Challenges and opinions

Complexity of institutions: The diversity and complexity of establishments make it difficult to create generic theories or fashions. Establishments can vary drastically throughout cultures and contexts, complicating efforts to generalize findings.

Empirical measurement: Measuring the effect of establishments on economic consequences poses methodological demanding situations. Developing reliable indicators for institutional first-class and performance is crucial for empirical analysis.

Integration with Mainstream Economics: Institutional economics regularly operates at the fringes of mainstream financial concept, main to problems in integrating its insights into traditional models. This marginalization can prevent its effect on broader economic policy discussions.

Policy Implications

Strengthening institutions: To foster economic development, policymakers ought to attention on strengthening establishments that promote transparency, duty, and efficiency. Reforms aimed toward enhancing belongings rights, reducing corruption, and improving the rule of law can contribute to higher financial consequences.

Tailored methods: Spotting the ancient and cultural context of institutions is important for designing effective policies. Policymakers should adopt tailored methods that recollect the precise institutional panorama and the needs of nearby groups.

Encouraging Collective movement: Selling collective movement and cooperation among stakeholders is vital for addressing complex financial and social demanding situations. Institutions that facilitate collaboration can beautify aid control, innovation, and social brotherly love.

Tracking and evaluation: Policymakers should implement mechanisms for tracking and comparing the impact of institutional reforms. Non-stop assessment can assist in becoming aware of what works and what does not, bearing in mind iterative enhancements in policy design.

To sum up, institutional economics provides a valuable framework for understanding the interaction among institutions and economic behaviour. By emphasising the role of institutions in shaping economic outcomes, this approach enriches our understanding of economic development, governance, and policy-making. As economies face an increasing number of complex challenges in a globalised world, the insights from institutional economics are critical for fostering sustainable growth and resilience. Embracing the principles of institutional economics can help policymakers navigate the intricacies of financial systems and promote effective institutional arrangements.

Evolutionary Economics

Evolutionary economics is a field that applies standards from evolutionary biology to understand monetary strategies and dynamics. This method focuses on the approaches in which monetary structures evolve over time, highlighting the roles of innovation, opposition, and institutional exchange. Unlike conventional monetary theories that often rely on equilibrium and rational decision-making, evolutionary economics emphasizes dynamic techniques, historical context, and the importance of social and institutional factors.

Ancient Context

The roots of evolutionary economics may be traced back to the early 20th century, with key figures including Thorstein Veblen, Joseph Schumpeter, and Ronald Coase contributing to its development. Veblen introduced the idea of "institutional economics," which examined the effect of social establishments on monetary conduct. Schumpeter emphasized the function of innovation and entrepreneurship in driving financial growth, coining the term "creative destruction" to describe how new improvements disrupt current markets. Coase's work on transaction costs similarly illustrated how institutional arrangements shape monetary sports.

Ideas of Evolutionary Economics

Dynamic processes: Evolutionary economics posits that monetary structures are not static but are constantly converting due to various factors, which includes technological improvements, shifts in customer alternatives, and changes inside the institutional environment. This dynamism makes it essential to look at economies over the years in preference to in static equilibrium states.

Innovation and Technological exchange: Innovation is an important subject in evolutionary economics. It is considered as a key driving force of monetary boom and structural change. The manner of innovation includes not only the development of new products and technology but also the adaptation of current ones. Evolutionary economists emphasize that innovation is frequently incremental and stimulated by the interactions among firms, industries, and establishments.

Natural selection in Economics: Borrowing from Darwinian ideas, evolutionary economics shows that firms and industries go through a form of natural selection. Successful companies that adapt to changing marketplace conditions survive and thrive, while those who fail to innovate or adapt may be pushed out of the marketplace. This competitive technique results in the evolution of industries over the years.

Course Dependence: Course dependence is an important concept in evolutionary economics, suggesting that ancient events and selections considerably impact the present and future trajectories of economic structures. Once a certain course is taken—along with the adoption of a particular generation or institutional arrangement—it can be difficult to shift to an alternative direction, even though the latter can be more efficient.

Institutional Frameworks: Institutions play an important position in shaping monetary conduct and results. Evolutionary economists argue that establishments—ranging from legal structures to cultural norms—affect how individuals and companies interact within the economic system. Institutional trade can cause new monetary practices and innovations, in addition to using the evolutionary system.

Programs of Evolutionary Economics

Economic boom and improvement: Evolutionary economics presents insights into the tactics that drive financial growth and development. By examining how technological change and innovation occur within unique contexts, this method facilitates explaining variations in growth rates across nations and regions.

Commercial Dynamics: The framework of evolutionary economics is used to research the dynamics of industries, including the emergence of new sectors and the decline of old ones. Understanding these dynamics is essential for policymakers seeking to foster innovation and competitiveness within their economies.

Policy Implications: Policymakers can utilize insights from evolutionary economics to design interventions that promote innovation and adaptability. For example, Research & Development (R&D) and supporting entrepreneurship can help create environments conducive to monetary evolution.

Sustainability and Environmental Economics: Evolutionary economics gives a framework for understanding the interactions among economic activities and environmental sustainability. By inspecting how economies adapt to ecological changes and constraints, this approach can inform strategies for sustainable development.

Challenges and evaluations

Complexity and Modeling: The dynamic and complex nature of evolutionary tactics makes it hard to develop formal models that capture these interactions. Critics argue that without specific modelling, the predictive power of evolutionary economics can be limited.

Integration with Mainstream Economics: Evolutionary economics often operates on the fringes of mainstream economic thought, leading to difficulties in integrating its insights into conventional monetary models. This marginalization can avert its effect on broader economic policy discussions.

Empirical Validation: Whilst evolutionary economics offers a rich theoretical framework, empirical validation of its standards can be difficult. Gathering data that captures the dynamic nature of economic evolution calls for progressive study methodologies.

Evolutionary economics gives a valuable perspective on understanding economic processes as dynamic and historically contingent. By emphasizing innovation, competition, and institutional change, this approach enriches our understanding of economic growth and development. As economies become increasingly complex and interconnected, insights from evolutionary economics could be crucial for informing powerful regulations that promote resilience, adaptability, and sustainability. Embracing the ideas of evolutionary economics can assist policymakers and researchers navigate the uncertainties of a rapidly changing economic landscape.

Religion & Economics

How Religion Can Boost Economic Growth in a Nation

With the aid of encouraging social belief, ethical behavior, and societal concord—all of which are important for financial increase—religion will have a good impact on a nation's financial system. Shared spiritual convictions frequently foster agree with among human beings, which lowers transaction expenses in commercial enterprise and fosters greater cordial financial dealings. In financial establishments and markets, belief is essential since it reduces the probability of fraud and corruption.

Religious teachings generally place a strong emphasis on ethical conduct, such as justice and honesty, which could enhance corporate operations and win over customers. Investments are drawn in and stable commercial enterprise environments are supported with the aid of this moral foundation. Further, a number of religions inspire altruism and network involvement, which may reduce inequality and poverty. Religious institutions assist social welfare by means of promoting charity, which improves human capital by means of providing better healthcare and schooling.

Additionally, spiritual festivals and activities can stimulate monetary interest by boosting tourism and local agencies. These activities now not only create jobs but also generate significant revenue for local economies. In precis, faith can offer a moral foundation, enhance social capital, and promote inclusive economic growth, making it a powerful force for economic development.

The Potential Benefits of Hindu Religion for India's Economy

The historic texts and highbrow traditions of the Hindu faith provide a one-of-a-kind viewpoint that can resource in the expansion and development of the modern-day Indian financial system. Long-term financial improvement dreams are aligned with the values of Hinduism, which are based on sustainable practices, communal well-being, ethical business practices, and balanced character progress. There are instructions discovered in Hindu literature, including the Vedas, Upanishads, Bhagavad Gita, Arthashastra, and Manu smriti, which are relevant to modern Indian financial practices.

Business and Ethics:

A foundation for moral leadership, judgment, and corporate ethics can be found in the Bhagavad Gita, one of the most well-known Hindu scriptures. The concept of dharma (duty) and karma(action), which emphasizes the significance of carrying out one's tasks without becoming unduly wedded to the results, is fundamental to the Gita. This can be translated for contemporary corporations into a focus on corporate social responsibility (CSR), where the community and stakeholders' well-being is prioritized over only profit.

Moral leadership, which inspires sustainability and long-term vision, can aid in preventing unethical practices and fostering trust in the enterprise atmosphere within the context of economic growth. The Gita's teaching that moral conduct is the course to prosperity might encourage company executives to follow ethical standards that advance the economic system and society as a whole. Moreover, corporations that encompass social responsibility into their commercial enterprise plans generally outperform their competition over the long term, strengthening the foundation of the economy.

Ecological Responsibility and Sustainability:

Hinduism has continually positioned a robust emphasis on the sacred bond between nature and humanity, seeing the earth (Prithvi) as a dwelling aspect that needs to be treated with reverence and care. The Upanishads and other historical writings, which include the Vedas, promote sustainable living through balancing monetary hobby with ecological concord.

For the reason that environmental deterioration is a major impediment to India's monetary development, this ideology is extremely pertinent. Over-exploitation of natural sources can end result from financial increase; however, this can be avoided via taking a sustainable strategy, which is burdened in Vedic literature. India can attain sustainable improvement without depleting its natural resources through including environmental sustainability into its improvement techniques. For instance, the developing renewable power industry in India fits in well with Hinduism's appreciate for the natural world. Promoting sustainable corporate practices also can attract overseas investment due to the fact environmental, social, and governance (ESG) concerns have become increasingly more vital in international marketplaces.

Economic Strategy and Financial Prudence: Considered to be one of the first writings on economics, the Arthashastra is an antique Indian literature on statecraft, monetary coverage, and army strategy that is credited to Kautilya (Chanakya). It addresses subjects associated with change, agriculture, public finance, taxation, and authorities while providing steerage on accountable spending. Current monetary guidelines can benefit from the software of the Arthashastra's precepts, particularly in the fields of taxation, resource control, and public spending. Maintaining a stability among governmental revenue and public welfare is important for sustainable economic progress, because the Arthashastra states. It promotes effective and equitable taxation whilst cautioning in opposition to excessive taxation, that could purpose monetary stagnation and public unrest. That is an example that modern India can use to restructure its tax laws, making them extra powerful and growth-oriented even as preserving the well-being of all societal segments.

Dharmic Principles and the Function of Community and Cooperation: Hindu teachings offer a sturdy emphasis on the significance of community and the common good, which could provide the groundwork for inclusive development. The concept of Sarva Loka Hitam, or "the well-being of all beings," promotes inclusive laws and business practices that benefit all aspects of society, particularly underprivileged groups.

The implementation of modern financial regulations can ensure that development spreads beyond urban areas to rural regions by cultivating a spirit of cooperation and collective duty. Hindu philosophy's tenet of shared prosperity can serve as a model for laws intended to reduce economic disparities and ensure that the most disadvantaged groups benefit financially. This philosophy is supported by programs like microfinance and cooperatives, which provide rural people and small-scale businesses more impact and have the capacity to spur tremendous economic growth.

Innovation and Skill Development: The Significance of Information: In Hinduism, education is noticeably valued, because the Upanishads portray education as a method of achieving self-attention. This cognizance on education may be applied to the modern Indian requirement for innovation and talent development, important additives of economic growth.

By making investments in education and skill development, India can create a hard work force that is competitive in the global economy. Moreover, the practice of gurukul (learning communities) might serve as an inspiration for current establishments to embrace comprehensive and resourceful coaching methodologies that foster creativity and critical thinking. The emphasis that the Indian government is putting on programmes like "Skill India" and "Digital India" is consistent with this historic emphasis on education and creativity.

Consumerism and Simplicity, Juggling Wealth and Spirituality: The Hindu ideal of modest life and accelerated awareness promotes a realistic mind-set in the direction of worldly prosperity. One of the four purusharthas (goals of existence) is money (artha), however different objectives, consisting of dharma (goodness) and moksha (spiritual freedom), continuously stability it out. This approach can fight the spread of consumerism and materialism, which frequently results in unsustainable habits and economic inequality.

Encouragement of moderation and minimalism can lead to extra responsible consumption habits, which is right for the economic system as a whole in addition to for people. Moreover, this might resource in addressing problems like debt accumulation, environmental deterioration, and social unrest. Hindu values can promote financial fashions that put the best of life above the pursuit of material wealth by promoting moderation in consumption.

To sum up, the rich legacy of Hindu philosophy and literature provides ageless steerage for the growth and advancement of the modern-day Indian economic system. India can create an economic system that isn't always only rich but also equitable and sustainable by using combining the moral precepts of the Bhagavad Gita, the Vedic sustainability principles, the Arthashastra's monetary techniques, and the numerous texts' emphasis on community welfare and education. Hinduism can continue to steer the growth in the twenty-first century, providing a moral and intellectual foundation for development.

Developing and Growing India's Economy: Present Strategies and Upcoming Courses

With a huge proportion of its population being young, strong domestic demand, and considerable economic Chas, India's economy has become one of the fastest-growing major economies in the world. But in order to maintain this growth and guarantee all-encompassing development, India must make efficient use of its current policies and enact new ones that deal with pressing issues. This essay examines the ways in which India's present policies can promote economic growth and make recommendations for new ones that will support long-term development.

Currently Adopting Measures to Encourage Economic Growth:

The Digital India Initiative: India's goal with the Digital India program is to become a knowledge economy and a society empowered by digital means. This policy has created new opportunities for online education, digital payments, and e-commerce by strengthening digital infrastructure and expanding internet access.

As an illustration, the Digital India initiative's Unified Payments Interface (UPI) has completely transformed digital payments in India by promoting financial inclusion and streamlining transactions. By processing more than 10 billion transactions a month by 2024, UPI will have proven how effective digital financial integration is in fostering entrepreneurship and economic activity, particularly in rural and semi-urban areas.

Make in India: Designed to position India as a global center for manufacturing, "Make in India" aims to raise the manufacturing sector's GDP share by enticing both domestic and foreign businesses to invest in the industry. The policy has assisted in lowering regulatory obstacles and improving infrastructure to draw in capital.

For instance, large manufacturing facilities built in India by international behemoths like Apple and Samsung have increased local production capacity and generated thousands of employment. For example, the manufacturing of mobile phones has experienced rapid expansion, making India the world's second-largest producer of mobile phones, with huge contributions to export revenue and GDP.

The GST (Goods and Services Tax): With the introduction of the Goods and Services Tax (GST), a unified tax system has been established, simplifying the tax code and facilitating cross-state corporate operations. This has expanded the tax base by lowering operating costs and raising compliance.

To illustrate, Prior to the introduction of GST, a truck transporting product across India had to stop at checkpoints for roughly 20% of the way, which caused delays and extra expenses. State-level taxes were removed with the implementation of the Goods and Services Tax (GST), which resulted in a 20% decrease in logistics costs and an increase in supply chain efficiency. This has facilitated the expansion of small firms' national marketplaces and attracted foreign investment by streamlining the tax procedure.

The "Self-Reliant India" or Aatmanirbhar Bharat campaign: The goal of this program is to increase local production capacities in a variety of areas, including as manufacturing, MSMEs, agriculture, and defence, in order to foster self-reliance. It seeks to create robust supply chains and lessen reliance on imports.

For instance, The COVID-19 pandemic highlighted the significance of independence in pharmaceuticals and medical supplies. India quickly increased the amount of personal protective equipment (PPE) kits and ventilators it was producing in order to meet both domestic and international demand. This change illustrates how self-reliance can improve economic growth and resilience.

Infrastructure Development: Building world-class infrastructure in areas including energy, urban development, and transportation is the goal of the National Infrastructure Pipeline (NIP) and other infrastructure initiatives. Costs are decreased, productivity is increased, and foreign direct investment is drawn to improved infrastructure (FDI).

As an illustration, the creation of the Delhi-Mumbai Industrial Corridor (DMIC) is expected to revolutionize local economies by bringing smart cities and high-speed freight connectivity. In order to show how infrastructure investment affects economic growth, this initiative seeks to double employment potential, treble industrial output, and quadruple exports from the area in the following five years.

Policy Suggestions for Long-Term Development and Growth

Although India's existing policies have created a strong basis for economic growth, there are a number of sectors in which new approaches and policy changes could further accelerate development.

Labour Market Reforms: Rigid laws that frequently discourage enterprises from growing and investing in formal employment are a defining feature of India's labour market. India should relax labour rules, increase hiring practices' flexibility, and give informal workers more social security in order to promote a more vibrant labour market.

An Example India might increase manufacturing and employment by implementing labour reforms akin to those in China's Special Economic Zones (SEZs), where accommodating labour regulations and incentives have drawn large FDI. These reforms may be able to draw in foreign corporations searching for locations outside of China, particularly in the context of global supply chain realignments.

Improving Human Capital: Developing a skilled workforce that can spur innovation and productivity requires significant investments in education and vocational training. Policies should prioritize raising the standard of education across the board, increasing access to postsecondary education, and coordinating skill development with business demands.

An example of a positive move is the National Education Policy (NEP) 2020, which places a strong emphasis on vocational training and transdisciplinary education. To guarantee that education translates into employability, more work must be done. India might learn from the effective integration of vocational training into school systems in nations like Germany in order to close the skills gap.

Reforms in Agriculture: India's economy still mostly depends on agriculture, albeit it suffers from low productivity and dispersed landholdings. Modernising agriculture through the use of new technologies, expanding financing availability, and creating effective supply chains should be the main goals of reforms.

An Example Contract farming can be successfully implemented nationwide if it is successful in places like Maharashtra and Punjab, where farmers receive guaranteed pricing and technical assistance from businesses. Enhancing crop diversification and decreasing reliance on crops that require a lot of water can also improve agriculture's sustainability and profitability.

Reforms in the Financial Sector: Strong financial institutions are essential for economic expansion. India has to prioritize lowering non-performing assets (NPAs), expanding financial inclusion, and enhancing loan availability, particularly for MSMEs.

For instance, the 2016 adoption of the Insolvency and Bankruptcy Code (IBC) represented a major change in how NPAs were addressed. To speed up the resolution procedure and strengthen the credit culture, more advancements are necessary. India might improve the efficiency of its financial sector operations and draw in more investment by taking cues from Singapore's well-functioning financial regulatory structure.

Sustainability of the Environment: For long-term sustainability, economic expansion and environmental preservation must be balanced. India ought to encourage the use of renewable energy sources, improve energy efficiency, and enact stronger environmental laws.

As an illustration, consider the International Solar Alliance (ISA), which India co-founded and is leading the way in promoting solar energy. India may make the shift to a greener economy easier by increasing incentives for green technologies and enforcing stronger pollution control regulations.

Export promotion and trade policy: India must increase competitiveness and diversify its export markets in order to increase exports. It is crucial to streamline trade laws, enhance logistics, and negotiate advantageous trade agreements.

For instance, India can learn from Vietnam's accomplishments in growing its exports through the negotiation of free trade agreements (FTAs) with powerful economies such as the US and the EU. Increasing the number of free trade agreements and lowering non-tariff barriers may allow Indian goods to enter new markets, especially in industries like IT services, pharmaceuticals, and textiles.

Smart Cities and Urbanization: Sustainable urban development policies are necessary given the rapid urbanization. Urban centers that are dynamic and stimulate economic growth can be achieved by extending the Smart Cities Mission and emphasizing sustainable planning, affordable housing, and effective public transportation.

For instance, India may learn a lot from Singapore's smart city model, which combines technology with environmentally friendly urban design. By implementing such methods, Indian towns may enhance resource management and offer superior living standards, thereby drawing in international talent and investment.

Fortifying Institutions and Governance: Strong institutions and effective governance are essential for long-term economic growth. India should prioritise lowering corruption, increasing ease of doing business, and boosting the effectiveness and transparency of public institutions.

For instance, India may be motivated to cut red tape and improve service delivery by the success of Estonia's e-governance model, in which the majority of public services are accessible online. Investor trust will also increase if the judiciary is strengthened to resolve disputes more quickly and enforce contracts more strictly.

Inclusive Growth and Reducing Inequality: Economic growth should be inclusive, ensuring that all sections of society benefit. Policies aimed at reducing income inequality, improving access to quality education and health care, and expanding social safety nets are essential.

For instance, the success of Brazil's Bolsa Família program, which provides conditional cash transfers to low-income families, has significantly reduced poverty and inequality. India could adopt similar targeted social welfare programs to ensure that economic growth benefits all sections of society, particularly the marginalized.

To sum up, India needs to take a multifaceted strategy to addressing changing difficulties, leveraging current policies and adopting new ones as needed, in order to achieve sustainable economic growth and development. India can establish a strong economic base by prioritizing digital transformation, manufacturing, infrastructure, and self-sufficiency. To realize its full economic potential, the nation must also give top priority to labour market reforms, human capital development, agricultural modernisation, financial sector improvement, environmental sustainability, and good governance. By putting these policies into practice, India will guarantee inclusive, resilient, and sustainable economic growth, establishing it as a major player in the world economy in the decades to come.

Wildlife-Integrated Economic Theory (WET)

The economic demanding situations of contemporary India encompass poverty, unemployment, environmental degradation, and an unbalanced development technique. Conventional financial theories frequently prioritize commercial increase and urbanization, sidelining the ecological and wildlife dimensions critical for long-time period sustainability. In this context, Wildlife-Integrated Economic Theory (WET) presents a unique approach through blending economics with flora and fauna conservation, presenting that natural world and ecological systems aren't just passive beneficiaries of economic rules but lively contributors to monetary prosperity.

The Essence of WET

WET is a pioneering economic idea that integrates wildlife conservation into mainstream economic strategies, arguing that retaining and enhancing wildlife habitats can function as a powerful financial engine. This idea is built on three main ideas:

Ecological Capitalism: This principle redefines traditional financial capital to include ecological capital, spotting wildlife and natural ecosystems as precious belongings that generate economic blessings. Ecological capitalism emphasises the sustainable use of wildlife sources, wherein wildlife habitats are controlled as living monetary property that generate earnings through tourism, environmental offerings, and biodiversity blessings.

Wildlife-economic system Nexus: This principle establishes an instantaneous link among wildlife conservation and financial increase, arguing that healthy ecosystems aid numerous industries such as agriculture, tourism, and fisheries. For instance, retaining wetlands can increase local fisheries, while keeping forests can enhance tourism and provide ecosystem services such as clean water and carbon sequestration.

Community-Centric Conservation: This precept emphasises involving neighbourhood groups in flora and fauna conservation efforts, ensuring that the financial blessings of conservation are equitably shared. Through empowering groups, WET seeks to create a sustainable balance between financial improvement and natural world protection, turning potential conflicts into synergies.

The reason behind WET

India's wealthy biodiversity, with its huge variety of flora and fauna, is an untapped aid with immense economic capability. WET acknowledges that flora and fauna and natural ecosystems are not just historical past assets but economic multipliers. Right here's why integrating flora and fauna into economic planning may be transformative for India:

Tourism revenue: India is home to numerous national parks, flora and fauna sanctuaries, and biosphere reserves that appeal to hundreds of thousands of tourists yearly. WET proposes investing in wildlife conservation to enhance the tourism sector, creating jobs and boosting local economies. For example, Ranthambore and Jim Corbett national Parks generate significant revenue through ecotourism, demonstrating the economic potential of well-managed wildlife reserves.

Surrounding services: Wildlife performs a crucial role in retaining ecosystem stability, which directly influences agricultural productivity, water resources, and weather regulation. WET emphasises defensive ecosystems like forests and wetlands, which act as carbon sinks, adjust water cycles, and aid biodiversity, thereby contributing to common financial balance.

Biodiversity and Agriculture: Flora and fauna contribute to agriculture through pollination, pest management, and maintaining soil fitness. By integrating WET, India can enhance agricultural productivity and food security, reducing dependence on chemical fertilizers and pesticides. For instance, maintaining bird populations that manage pests can reduce crop losses, benefiting farmers economically.

Sustainable Livelihoods: WET promotes sustainable livelihoods through linking conservation efforts with local economic activities. Groups living close to flora and fauna habitats can engage in sustainable practices including beekeeping, natural farming, and handicrafts, reducing their dependence on harmful activities like poaching and deforestation.

Implementation strategies for WET

Policy Integration: Integrate wildlife conservation into countrywide and nation-degree financial rules. This includes mandating environmental impact assessments that take into account the economic cost of wildlife habitats before approving development projects.

Public-private Partnerships: Encourage partnerships between the authorities, private sector, and local groups to fund wildlife conservation initiatives. For instance, private groups can invest in ecotourism ventures that benefit both flora and fauna and local economies.

Community-based Conservation packages: Develop packages that involve neighbourhood groups in conservation efforts, offering economic incentives for maintaining flora and fauna habitats. This can be carried out through schemes like network-managed tourism, natural world safaris, and conservation agriculture.

Wildlife-related economic instruments: Introduce monetary instruments consisting of green bonds and natural world conservation price range that channel investments into wildlife safety and habitat recuperation. These instruments can provide an opportunity for revenue generation for conservation efforts.

Education and awareness: Launch educational campaigns to raise awareness about the monetary cost of wildlife conservation. Educating citizens about the benefits of wildlife can foster a culture of conservation, making it a mainstream economic priority.

Ability advantages of WET for India.

Economic increase: By harnessing wildlife as an economic asset, India can generate huge sales via tourism, sustainable agriculture, and ecosystem offerings. This technique can assist in diversifying the economic system and decreasing reliance on conventional business sectors.

Activity advent: WET can create hundreds of thousands of jobs in wildlife control, ecotourism, conservation agriculture, and related fields. This is especially essential in rural regions, where employment possibilities are constrained.

Environmental Sustainability: WET promotes sustainable financial practices that uphold biodiversity, reduce carbon footprints, and mitigate the effects of climate change. This aligns with India's commitments to international environmental agreements and sustainable development goals.

Stepped forward best of life: By way of protective ecosystems that provide clean water, air, and food, WET enhances the quality of life for communities. Access to nature-based recreational activities also improves mental and physical health.

Cultural preservation: Natural world conservation is deeply connected to India's cultural history. WLT helps with the maintenance of traditional information and practices that recognise and defend nature, fostering a sense of nationwide pride.

Demanding situations and Mitigation strategies

Warfare of pursuits: Balancing economic development and flora and fauna conservation can result in conflicts, particularly in areas where land is scarce. WET indicates zoning and land-use planning that prioritises conservation in ecologically sensitive regions while promoting sustainable development elsewhere.

Investment Constraints: Flora and fauna conservation regularly face funding demanding situations. WET proposes modern financing mechanisms, such as ecotourism levies and natural world-linked bonds, to secure sustainable investment sources.

Resistance from nearby groups: Network resistance to conservation efforts can rise if financial advantages aren't currently seen. WET advocates for transparent advantage-sharing mechanisms to ensure that groups see tangible rewards from conservation.

Lack of awareness: Educating stakeholders, which includes policymakers, businesses, and most people, about the financial value of wildlife is crucial. WET recommends integrating conservation education into school curricula and public campaigns.

To sum up, Theory is a groundbreaking framework that reimagines the function of wildlife in India's monetary development. By integrating wildlife conservation into economic planning, WET not only addresses environmental concerns but also unlocks new economic possibilities, fostering sustainable growth. This revolutionary approach positions India as a global leader in balancing economic progress with ecological maintenance, ensuring a rich and sustainable future for all.

References

1. Acamoglu, D., & Robinson, J. A. (2012). Why Nation Fails: The Origins of Power, prosperity, and Poverty. Crown Business.
2. Arthashastra: R. P. Kangle (1992). "The Kautilya Arthashastra". Motilal Banarsidass.
3. Bhagavad Gita: Eknath Easwaran (2007). "The Bhagavad Gita". Nilgiri Press.
4. Chapra, M. U. (1992). Islam and the economic challenge. Islamic Foundation.
5. Crone, Patricia. "Pre-Industrial Societies: Anatomy of the Pre-Modern World."
6. Environmental and Natural Resource Economics: A Contemporary Approach"* by Jonathan M. Harris and Brian Roach
7. Kahneman, D., & Tversky, A. (1979). Prospect theory: An analysis of decision under risk. Econometrica, 47(2), 263–291.
8. Kalecki, M. (1971). Selected Essays on the Dynamics of the Capitalist Economy. Cambridge University Press.
9. Keynes, J. M. (1936). The General Theory of Employment, Interest, and Money. Harcourt, Brace and Company.
10. Krugman, P., & Wells, R. (2020). Microeconomics (5th ed.). Worth Publishers.
11. Lenin, Vladimir. The State and Revolution. New York: Penguin Books, 1992 (originally published in 1917).
12. Lowry, S. Todd. "The Archaeology of Economic Ideas: The Classical Greek Tradition."
13. Luxemburg, Rosa. The Accumulation of Capital. New York: Routledge, 2003 (originally published in 1913).

14. Mankiw, N. G.(2020). Principles of Microeconomics (9th ed.).

15. Marx, Karl, and Friedrich Engels. The Communist Manifesto. London: Penguin Books, 2002 (originally published in 1848).

16. Marx, Karl. Das Kapital: A Critique of Political Economy. Volume I. London: Penguin Classics, 1992 (originally published in 1867).

17. Nelson, R. R., & Winter, S. G. (1982). An Evolutionary Theory of Economic Change. Harvard University Press.

18. North, D. C. (1990). Institutions, Institutional Change and Economic Performance. Cambridge University Press.

19. Osborne, M. J., & Rubinstein, A. (1994). A Course in Game Theory.

20. Publisher: Barnes & Noble Books, 1985.

21. Publisher: Duke University Press, 1987.

22. Publisher: Oneworld Publications, 2003.

23. Publisher: Oxford University Press, 1954.

24. Schumpeter, Joseph A. "History of Economic Analysis."

25. Silver, Morris. "Economic Structures of the Ancient Near East."

26. Snyder, D. R., & L. F. (2001). Chaos Theory in the Social Sciences: Foundations and Applications. University of Michigan Press.

27. Thaler, R. H., & Sunstein, C. R. (2008). *Nudge: Improving decisions about

28. Upanishads: Patrick Olivelle (1998). "The Early Upanishads: Annotated Text and Translation". Oxford University Press.

29. Vedas: David Frawley (2000). "The Rig Veda and the History of India". Aditya Prakashan.